Promoting Tourism in India: A Case Study

PROMOTING TOURISM IN INDIA A CASE STUDY

Dr. Kranti P. Sawarkar
Subodh Kumar Mishra

KANISHKA PUBLISHERS, DISTRIBUTORS
NEW DELHI-110 002

KANISHKA PUBLISHERS, DISTRIBUTORS
4697/5-21 A, Ansari Road, Daryaganj
New Delhi-110 002
Phones : 2327 0497, 2328 8285
Fax : 011-2328 8285
E-mail: kanishka_publishing@yahoo.co.in

Promoting Tourism in India: A Case Study

First Published 2010

ISBN 978-81-8457-163-9

PRINTED IN INDIA

Published by Madan Sachdeva for Kanishka Publishers, Distributors, 4697/5-21A, Ansari Road, Daryaganj, New Delhi-110 002, Typeset by Sunshine Graphics, Delhi, and Printed at Rajdhani Printers, Delhi.

Preface

India is a land of all seasons and for all reasons. Hardly any country in the world can match the diversity India portrays. However for years, the flow of inbound clients was restricted to few states like Rajasthan, Goa and Kerala. This trend was further emulated by the domestic travelers. As a result, there was a lot of pressure on the carrying capacity of the region. The need of the hour is to give the travelers alternative destinations. Thus comes the Vidarbha region in Central India. The untapped glories of this untouched terrain includes – Zero mile, the geographical centre of India; World's largest hyper velocity impact crater in basaltic rock; Best variety of oranges grown in India; social activists of national importance like *Acharya Vinoba Bhave, Baba Amte, Saint Gajanan Maharaj, Saint Gadge Bab;* Four National Parks and 14 Wild Life Sanctuaries; and the scenic spot that inspired the Great Poet *Kalidasa* to write epics – to name a few.

However to give Vidarbha its due place in the tourist map of India and the world, we need a right development road map coupled with concerted efforts by state and central government. There is a need to evaluate where we stand today and how do we proceed from here. This book attempts to do exactly the same. It depicts the geographic and touristic personality of Vidarbha, enlist places that have touristic appeal and also evaluate the currents facilities. At the end, it provides a complete road map for systematic development of Vidarbha into a major tourist hub of inbound as well as domestic clients. This will serve as a pioneer study on this region and encourage further research on the touristic appeal of this region.

The book starts dealing with the conceptual frame-work of tourism, its growth in present, past and future perspectives, and tourism potential of India. The historical background takes us on a journey down the timeline of Vidarbha. Thereafter the geographic personality of the region gives the physical features, topography, weather phenomenon, forest and mineral resources, population and settlement, education, economy and the like aspects. But perhaps the most important section of this book is the one which sketches the touristic personality of Vidarbha region. It has been further sub divided into man-made tourist attractions and the natural tourist places. It also paints the kaleidoscope of the beautiful living culture of this region i.e. traditional performing art like dance, drama; music – vocal and instrumental; tribal and folk culture; fairs and festivals; costume, cuisine and the like topics. A description of the existing tourist infrastructure and traffic trends is included. While giving the current resource use pattern, it enlists and evaluates the resource potential. Unique Selling Point (USP) of the region that can act as a catalyst for fuelling the tourism promotion in the region, also finds as mentioned in the book.

At the same time it reviews the ongoing efforts by private and public sector enterprises making a critical evaluation of government policies. Further it enlists the strengths, weakness, opportunities and threats. The book also chalks out a strategy for tourism promotion in the Vidarbha region. The strategy includes identification of priority market, infrastructure development, local participation, training and awareness. Last but not the least; it discusses ideas for promotional campaigns that can give Vidarbha its justified place in the tourist map of India.

Dr. Kranti P. Sawarkar
Subodh Kumar Mishra

Contents

1
Introduction

Since the dawn of civilization tourism has been the 'basic instinct' of human beings, and India, being mother of all civilizations, has a long history of tourism on its soil. Archeological excavations prove that Harappan civilization had a well-developed dockyard and even maintained a steady trade relation with contemporary civilizations overseas. Thus, international tourism was a regular feature in India some 5000 years ago. Ideologically, Indians consider serving a guest as a pious activity. A tenet in Sanskrit goes like this–"*Atithi Devo Bhav.*" It means "Guest is the God Himself." Domestic tourism attained great heights when the benevolent emperors like *Samrat Asoka* understood the importance of tourism and erected sound infrastructure for the ease of travellers including free service of food and shelter. They also encouraged scholars from foreign countries to visit India and thus we had Meghasthenes from Greece, Alberuni from Persia, Huen Tsang and Fa-Hien from China to name a few. Strongly motivated by 'curiosity' and 'quest for knowledge', these inquisitive souls, despite their limited means, used to set out on long and arduous journeys, bravely facing the en-route risks and discomforts. Their accounts on the life and people of India induced a strong urge in others to visit India. Also those travel accounts today have become an important source of Indian history.

In the beginning of the nineteenth century, tourism meant a pastime and thus a trivial activity. Today, one and a half centuries later, it is world's fastest growing industry having far-reaching socio-economic effects. Undoubtedly, the origin of modern tourism and its speedy growth can be attributed to the remarkable achievements in the field of science and technology. With the information revolution at its peak one can take a virtual tour of the world at the click of a button. Thus, technology creates both awareness and curiosity to travel to alien destinations. Secondly, the advent of cheaper and faster means of transport has removed the time and cost barrier to travel. Thirdly, greater automation at workplace has made tourism both convenient and compulsive. On one hand, it has provided more disposable income and leisure time. On the other, it has created an urge to escape from the drudgeries of monotonous city life. The ever-rising number of players, private as well as public, in the tourism industry has made it very competitive in terms of quality of services and their price. They are vying with each other to attract each additional tourist. The effective marketing strategies have certainly made customer the king and he has a number of alternatives to choose from.

Tourism and its Significance

Tourism is essentially an expression of natural human instinct for experience, education and entrainment. The motivation for tourism includes social, religion and business interests. The economic consequences of this phenomenon are wide-ranging and capable of influencing the development process of several nations, regions, societies and to a great extent of individuals. The increasingly recognized human, social, economic and cultural values of tourism need focused attention. Tourism contributes positively to reconciling environment protection, economic development and fight against poverty by creating wealth through foreign exchange earnings, contributions to national income and Government revenues, spreading of economic and social benefits to under-developed areas, income, job creation (particularly to women and disadvantaged groups), increased living standards and preservation and conservation of natural and cultural environment.

Over the years, tourism development has emerged as human centered, equitable and environmentally sustainable, thus contributing substantially to the philosophy of sustainable human development in both words and in actual practice, in reality, on ground, throughout the globe. At the same time, tourism can favour openness to international trade, technology innovation and protection of social and cultural identities.

At the start of the new millennium, tourism is firmly established as the number one industry in many countries and the fastest-growing economic sector in terms of foreign exchange earnings and job creation.

International tourism is the world's largest export earner and an important factor in the balance of payments of most nations. Tourism has become one of the world's most important sources of employment. It stimulates enormous investment in infrastructure, most of which also helps to improve the living conditions of local people. It provides governments with substantial tax revenues. Most new tourism jobs and business are created in developing countries, helping to equalize economic opportunities and keep rural residents from moving to overcrowded cities.

Intercultural awareness and personal friendships fostered through tourism are a powerful force for improving international understanding and contributing to peace among all the nations of the world.

The WTO recognizes that tourism can have a negative cultural, environmental and social impact if it is not responsibly planned, managed and monitored. The WTO thus encourages governments to play a vital role in tourism, in partnership with the private sector, local authorities and non-governmental organizations.

In its belief that tourism can be effectively used to address the problems of poverty, WTO made a commitment to contribute to the United Nations Millennium Development Goals through a new initiative to develop sustainable tourism as a force for poverty elimination. The programme, known as STEP (Sustainable Tourism-Eliminating Poverty), focuses the longstanding work of both organizations on encouraging sustainable tourism with a view to alleviating poverty and was implemented in 2003.

Economic Benefits of Tourism

- International tourism is the *world's largest export earner* and an important factor in the balance of payments of many countries.

- Tourism is an *important job creator*, employing millions of people around the world.
- *Rural Opportunities:* Tourism jobs and businesses are usually created in the most underdeveloped regions of a country, helping to equalize economic opportunities throughout a nation and providing an incentive for residents to remain in rural areas rather than move to overcrowded cities.
- Travel and tourism stimulates enormous *investments in new infrastructure*, most of which helps to improve the living conditions of local residents as well as tourists.
- The tourism industry provides governments with *hundreds of millions of dollars in tax revenues* each year.

But significance is not just economic...the *environment and local culture* receive a boost when authorities restore monuments, open museums and establish natural parks to lure visitors. As tourism increases, so does a destination's need to improve infrastructure to handle the influx. New airports, roads, marinas, sewage and water treatment plants and dozens of other projects are the result, providing a *substantial improvement in the residents' own lives* from cleaner drinking water to speedier communications.

And most important of all: tourism is a *human story*... it enriches with culture, environmental and social awareness, helps families to spend time together, brings openness and friendliness, be it on leisure or work. Tourism promotes peace and cooperation among nations and builds bridges.

Tourism Trends

In economic terms, international tourism receipts are classified as exports and international tourism expenditure as imports. For many countries, international tourism is an indispensable source of foreign-currency earnings.

According to the WTTC estimates, tourism represents 8.3 per cent of the global workforce. It plays a major role in the global economy and represents a significant global gross national product (GNP). Tourism is a highly fragmented industry with many different participants including tour operators, the transport and hotel industry, and of course, the tourists themselves. At the start of the 90's decade, several trends were observed at the global level. According to the report of the UN World Tourism Organization, 2008, Asia and the Pacific was the world's second best performing region in terms of arrivals in 2007 after the Middle East, recording an increase by 10 per cent to 184 million arivals. At the same time tourists were diversifying into highly specialized groups from among a broad range of activities. Increased interest in travel to natural and less disturbed areas due to a rapidly growing interest in environmental matters and nature was perceived as one of the trends. This was expected to result in an increased interest in Asia and tropical America, areas that still contained large tracts of wilderness.

According to world tourism organization, the share of Europe and America, in terms of world arrivals has gone down from 68.2 per cent and 25.5 per cent in 1970 to 53.6 per cent and 15.7 per cent and in terms of tourism receipt from 61.6 per cent and 26.8 per cent to 50.6 per cent and 19.9 per cent in 2007, respectively.

On the other hand the share of south and east Asia along with pacific region is consistently on rise, i.e. as against 3.7 per cent of world arrivals and 6.7 per cent of international receipts in 1970 its share increased to 20.4 per cent and 22 per cent respectively in 2007. But India has failed to take advantage of this boom in the tourism industry. India received a meager 0.56 per cent of total world tourist arrival and 1.25 per cent of world tourist receipts in 2007.

Until the UN World Tourism Organization and WTTC recently highlighted its economic benefits, tourism was generally regarded as a source of leisure and adventure and largely for the elite. It was not regarded as a global instrument to reduce poverty, apparently because government was not aware of the mammoth contribution tourism could make to economies.

The WTO statistics show that over the last 10 years, the annual growth of tourist arrival in developing countries and the LDC 74s (least developed countries) has been higher than the world average. The mark growth of international tourism receipts in the 49 LDC's, in particular, which account for 10.7 per cent of the world population but only 1.5 per cent of global wealth, was significant in the nineties. Tourism is an important export for one third of them. In 2000 developing countries recorded 292.6 million international arrivals, an increase of nearly 95 per cent when compared with the 1990 tally.

Furthermore in the LDC's there has been a 75 per cent increase in international arrivals, in the past decade. The United Nation Conference on Trade and Development (UNCTAD) points out that tourism is the main source of foreign exchange earnings for the 49 LDC's. A recent WTTC study on tourism's impact on the Indian economy shows that the travel and tourism industry generated Rs. 1,400 billion of economic activity in 2002, which is projected to grow to Rs. 6,582 billion by the year 2012, an impressive 9.7 per cent per annum growth. The travel and tourism economy's contribution (T&T) to the gross domestic product (GDP) was expected to increase from 4.8 per cent in 2002 to 5.5 per cent by 2012. But India achieved the 5.5 per cent mark in 2007 itself.

Similarly, T&T economy is expected to register a healthy rise in employment generation from 23.6 million in 2002 to 30.6 million in 2012. The study says T&T generated 6.5 per cent of total export (Rs. 205.9 billion) in 2002,which is expected to go up to Rs. 1,397 billion (7.9% of total) in 2012.

As far as capital investment is concerned, it is expected to grow from Rs. 356.5 billion in 2002 to Rs. 1,389.9 billion in 2012. In countries like India, tourism has not only become a primary source of foreign exchange earning, but has also provided one of the few options for diversifying the economy from the declining agriculture-based on.

Tourism 2020 Vision

Tourism 2020 Vision is the World Tourism Organization's long-term forecast and assessment of the development of tourism up to the first 20 years of the new millennium. An essential outcome of the Tourism 2020 Vision are quantitative forecasts covering a 25 years period, with 1995 as the base year and forecasts for 2000, 2010 and 2020.

WTO's Tourism 2020 Vision forecasts that international arrivals are expected to reach over 1.56 billion by the year 2020. Of these worldwide arrivals in 2020, 1.18 billion will be intraregional and 0.38 billion will be long-haul travellers.

International Tourist Arrivals by Receiving Region Growth Rate, 1955-2000

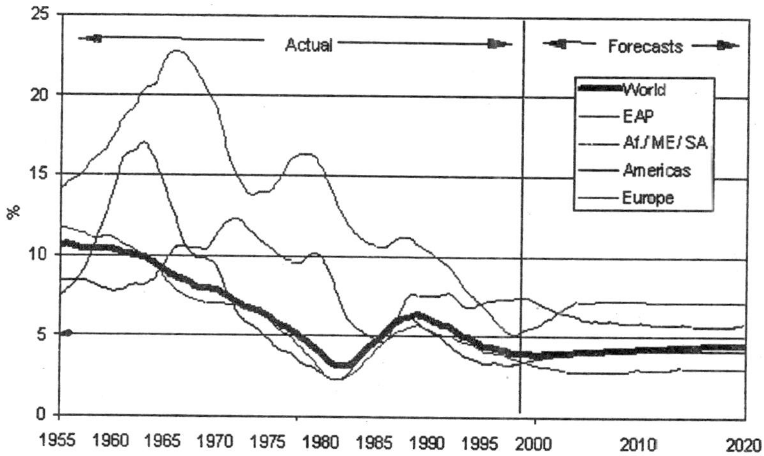

Source: World Tourism Organisation [WTO]©.

The total tourist arrivals by region shows that by 2020 the top three receiving regions will be Europe (717 million tourists), East Asia and the Pacific (397 million) and Americas (282 million), followed by Africa, the Middle East and South Asia.

East Asia and the Pacific, South Asia, the Middle East and Africa are forecasted to record growth at rates of over 5 per cent per year, compared to the world average of 4.1 per cent. The more mature regions Europe and Americas are anticipated to show lower than average growth rates.

Europe will maintain the highest share of world arrivals, although there will be a decline from 60 per cent in 1995 to 46 per cent in 2020. By 2010 the Americas will lose its number two position to the East Asia and the Pacific region which will receive 25 per cent of world arrivals in 2020 with the Americas decreasing from 19 per cent in 1995 to 18 per cent in 2020.

Long-haul travel worldwide will grow faster, at 5.4 per cent per year over the period 1995-2020, than intraregional travel, at 3.8 per cent. Consequently the ratio between intraregional and long haul travel will shift from around 82:18 in 1995 to close to 76:24 in 2020.

WTO Tourism 2020 Vision: Forecast of Inbound Tourism, World by Regions International Tourist Arrivals by Trouist Receiving Region (Million)

	Base Year	*Forecasts*		*Average Annual Growth Rate (%)*	*Market Share*	
	1995	*2010*	*2020*	*1995-2020*	*1995*	*2020*
World	565.4	1,004.4	1,561.1	4.1	100	100
Africa	20.2	47.0	77.3	5.5	3.6	5.0
Americas	108.9	190.4	282.3	3.9	19.3	18.1
East Asia and the Pacific	81.4	195.2	397.2	6.5	14.4	25.4
Europe	338.4	527.3	717.0	3.0	59.8	45.9
Middle East	12.4	35.9	68.5	7.1	2.2	4.4
South Asia	4.2	10.6	18.8	6.2	0.7	75.8
Intraregional (a)	464.1	790.9	1,183.3	3.8	82.1	75.8
Long-Haul (b)	101.3	215.5	377.9	5.4	17.9	24.2

Source: World Tourism Organization (WTO)©, (Actual data as in WTO database July 2000).

Notes: *(a)* Intraregional indudes arrivals where country of origin is not specified.

(b) Long-Haul is defined as everything except intraregional Travel.

Tourism Potential of India

That India has enormous tourism potential is a well-known fact. World-known historical monuments, temples, snow-clad bmountains, beautiful towering Himalayas, intriguing Ladakh, astonishingly beautiful Kashmir, Garhwal, and Himachal Pradesh, the serene Ganges basin, the lazy backwaters of Kerala, the cool heights of Darjeeling and Sikkim, rich wildlife of Sundarbans, the picturesque plateau of Deccan, the palm-fringed beaches of Goa, and not to talk about Taj Mahal or Khajuraho – India is in fact a unique country in the world. In fact, India is not a country; it is sub-continent. From North to South and East to West, the people are different, the languages are different, the customs are different, and the country is different. There are few countries on the earth with such an enormous variety that India has to offer. A distinguished foreign delegate in the 51st Annual Conference of Pacific-Asia Travel Association (held in New Delhi) rightly remarked, "There's no country in the world where you can experience this amazing diversity of food, culture, festival and of course, people."

India has the potential to release foreign exchange earnings of over $10 billion and attract 10 million tourists by 2010, even with the existing infrastructure, marginal investment in certain specific segments, rational management of hospitality industry and change in mindset of various players in the field. But where do we stand now? India's share in World tourist arrivals and receipts is dismally negligible. What is more appalling is that we are far below such small countries like Taiwan, Malaysia, Thailand, Korea, Indonesia, etc.

It is note worthy that China ranked fifth in the world's top 40 tourism earning countries, with external funds inflow of $42.9 billion, while India's rank was 42 with an international tourism receipt of little over $10 billion in 2007. While there has been substantial increase, both in terms of tourist arrivals and receipts the world and over, India's position was stagnant at about 0.5 per cent. Despite these unimpressive figures of India's share, *there are certain built in positive factors.* These include average duration of stay, (about one month), repeat visitors (42%), leisure tourist (58%) comparatively higher percentage of visitors being in the age group of 25-44 years, normally high spending category, increase in the proportion of business travellers etc.

The World Travel and Tourism Council (WTTC) estimates that contribution of the hospitality industry to Indian GDP is expected to go up to 6.6 per cent by 2010 and foreign exchange receipts from 10.8 per cent to 12 per cent of the aggregate exporter earnings in the same period. Given a thrust and determination it is possible to exceed the rate of growth of 8.43 per cent on arrivals projected by WTTC.

Notwithstanding our vast tourism potential, our performance, on this score is far from satisfactory. Of the 903 million tourists all over the world during 2007, a mere 0.56 per cent arrived in India. It is really a pity that India earns less than half of what other countries earn with less than half of tourist attractions than ours. For example, in 2007, city Nations like Hong Kong and Singapore earned $13.7 billion and $8.6 billion respectively from tourism as against our tourism earning of $10.7 billion in the same year. No doubt, tourism industry is one of the largest foreign exchange earners in our country. However, our rank is almost the last in the list of tourism destinations in the world. As of today, only one out of 250 tourists worldwide finds his/her destination in India.

Recent years have witnessed a phenomenal rise in the role and importance of tourism. Ex Prime Minister Shri Atal Bihari Vajpayee believed at tourism is a panacea for many ills. Addressing the 51st Annual Conference of Pacific-Asia Travel Association (PATA) in Delhi's Ashok Hotel, he said:

> *"Where as terrorism feeds on intolerance and arrogance, tourism breeds tolerance and empathy. Terrorism seeks to erect walls of hatred between faiths and communities; tourism breaks such barriers. Terrorism detests pluralism, whereas tourism pays tributes to it."*

This is precisely why, tourism is no longer considered as the luxurious private affair of a privileged few. It has instead, emerged as the fastest growing industry of the world over the past ten years. In the year 2007, global turnover of tourism industry was worth $856 billion, involving as many as 903 million people crossing international boundaries. In 2007, tourism accounted for more than 30 per cent of international trade in services, 8 per cent of world exports and 10.6 per cent of global employment. Prompted largely by such a phenomenal growth of this industry, many authorities in this field have now started terming it as a full-fledged sector. 'Hospitality Sector', as it is fashionably phrased today, is predicted to generate as much as $8613.8 billion, contributing 3.8 per cent of global GDP and creating 91 million jobs by 2012.

Realizing the multifarious benefits of tourism *vis-a-vis* its growth potential, more and more countries are now putting their best efforts to promote tourism, in a big way. India too is consistently vying to make its rightful place on the international map of tourism which is aptly evidently from the importance being given to this smokeless industry in country's overall planning.

India's Status in International Tourist Arrivals and Receipts in Past 3 years

Foreign Tourist Arrivals

Month	*Foreign Tourist Arrivals (Nos.)*			*Percentage Change*	
	2006	2007	2008 @	2007-06	2008-07
January	459489	535631	591337	16.6%	10.4%
February	439090	501692	561393	14.3%	11.9%
March	391009	472494	541478	20.8%	14.6%
April	309208	350550	384203	13.4%	9.6%
May	255008	277017	300840	8.6%	8.6%
June	278370	310364	340159	11.5%	9.6%
July	337332	399866	429456	18.5%	7.4%
August	304387	358446	391423	17.8%	9.2%
September	297891	301892	330874	1.3%	9.6%
October	391399	444564	452566	13.6%	1.8%
Total	**3463183**	**3952516**	**4323729**	**14.1%**	**9.4%**

Foreign Exchange Earnings in Rs. Crore

Month	*Foreign Exchange Earnings (In Rs. Crore)*			*Percentage Change*	
	*2006	2007*	2008#	2007-06	2008-07
January	3970	4698	5438	18.3%	15.8%
February	3793	4401	5182	16.0%	17.7%

Contd...

Month	*Foreign Exchange Earnings (In Rs. Crore)*			*Percentage Change*	
	*2006	2007*	2008#	2007-06	2008-07
March	3378	4144	5035	22.7%	21.5%
April	2850	3218	3773	12.9%	17.2%
May	2350	2543	2988	8.2%	17.5%
June	2566	2849	3409	11.0%	19.7%
July	2990	3436	3870	14.9%	12.6%
August	2698	3080	3626	14.2%	17.7%
September	2640	2594	3143	-1.7%	21.2%
October	3355	3785	4248	12.8%	12.2%
Total	**30590**	**34748**	**40712**	**13.6%**	**17.2%**

Foreign Exchange Earnings in US$ Million

Month	*Foreign Exchange Earnings (in US$ Million)*			*Percentage Change*	
	2006*	2007*	2008#	2007-06	2008-07
January	894	1064	1382	19.0%	29.9%
February	854	996	1305	16.6%	31.0%
March	761	938	1248	23.3%	33.0%
April	627	780	943	24.4%	20.9%
May	517	617	711	19.3%	15.2%
June	564	691	796	22.5%	15.2%
July	645	848	904	31.5%	6.6%
August	582	760	845	30.6%	11.2%
September	569	640	689	12.5%	7.7%
October	746	959	873	28.6%	-9.0%
Total	**6759**	**8293**	**9696**	**22.7%**	**16.9%**

@ Provisional Estimates * Revised Estimates # Advance Estimates.

Yet another remarkable trend in favor of India is that the average length of stay per tourist (around 30 days) is one of the highest in the world. Moreover, according to conservative estimates, tourism, tourism presently is providing employment opportunities to more than 8 million people in its direct sector. It becomes all the more important, since the employment multiplier in tourism sector comes to be about 2.36, i.e. direct employment to one person in tourism industry creates employment for 1.36 person in other sector of the economy. Not only this, the labour–capital ratio (at 1985-86 prices) is far higher in tourism sector (at 4.75) compared to manufacturing at 12.7 agriculture 44.7 and transport and other sector at 13.8 per cent (International Tourism Report–1996).

Vidarbha—A Historical Background

Vidarbha as a Kingdom has been in existence from time immemorial. Said to be established as his Kingdom by King Vidarbha, son of Rishabhadeva with Kaundinyapura as its capital, its queen Lopamudra finds mention in the Vedas (Rigveda hymn 1179,4). Vidarbha as a Kingdom is known since Bramhana and Upanishad times to the ancient Hindus. Uttarakanda of Ramayana mentions that Danda, son of Ikshwaku ruled over Vidarbha which then ranged from Vindhya to Shaivala. Mahabharata tells of its Princess Rukmini marrying Lord Krishna. In later times Maurya, Satavahana, Vakataka and Rashtrakuta and many other dynasties ruled over Vidarbha over time.

Nagpur the commercial center of Vidarbha, is believed to be settled by Gond King Bhakt Bulanda of Devgad around early 18th century. The control later passed on to the Bhosale dynasty. Vidarbha consisted of the Western part comprising of Amaravati, Akola, Yavatmal and Buldhana districts known as Varhad and Eastern part comprising of Nagpur, Bhandara, Wardha and Chandrapur district was the Kingdom of Devgad of the Gond Kings. The kingdom of Bhosale was lost to the British in 1853 A.D. In 1861 Nagpur became capital of Central Provinces. After independence the state of C.P. and Berar came in to being, with Nagpur as its capital. Later it became capital of Madhya Pradesh with the addition of Mahakoshal and Chhattisgarh region.

In 1960, though the Fazal Ali Commission for state reorganization had recommended creation of a separate state of

Vidarbha, it was merged in the state of Maharashtra with the status of second capital.

Ancient History

The oldest vestiges of Habitation in the Nagpur District are furnished by dolmens and other sepulchral monuments which can be noticed within a radius of about 48,280 km. (thirty miles) round Nagpur in the vicinity of the villages of Koradi, Kohali, Janapani, Nidhoa, Borganv, Vathora, Vadganv, Savarganv, Hingana etc. Some of these were opened first by Pearson and then by Hislop but their detailed reports are not available. They require to be excavated and studied scientifically. Hislop describes them as follows:

> *"They are found chiefly as barrows surrounded by a circle of stones, and as stone boxes, which when complete are styled kistvaens, and when open on one side, cromlechs. The kistvaens, if not previously disturbed, have been found to contain stone coffins and urns."*

Such sepulchral monuments are generally found to contain copper and bronze weapons, tools and earthen vessels. Some scholars find in these copper and bronze objects traces of the migration route of the Vedic Aryans. This culture is supposed to be later than that of the Indus Valley, of which no traces have yet been noticed in Vidarbha.

With the advent of the Aryans we get more light on the past history of this region. It was then covered by a thick jungle. Agastya was the first Aryan who crossed the Vindhya and fixed his hermitage on the bank of the Godavari. This memorable event is commemorated in the mythological story which represents Vindhya as blending before his guru Agastya when the latter approached him. The sage asked the mountain to remain in that condition until he returned from the south, which he never did. Agastya was followed by several other sages, who established their hermitages in different regions of the south. They were constantly harassed by the original inhabitants who are called Raksasas in the Ramayana. "These shapeless and ill-looking monsters testify their abominable character by various cruel and terrific displays.

They implicate the hermits in impure practices and perpetrate the greatest outrages. Changing their shapes and hiding in the thickets adjoining the hermitages, these frightful beings delight in terrifying the devotees. They cast away the sacrificial ladles and vessels; they pollute the cooked oblations, and utterly defile the offerings with blood. These faithless creatures inject frightful sounds into the ears of the faithful and austere hermits. At the time of the sacrifice they snatch away the jars, the flowers, the fuel and the sacred grass of these sober-minded man."

In course of time a large kingdom was founded in this region by king Vidarbha, the son of Rsabhadeva. His capital was Kindinapura in The Amravati district, which is still known by its ancient name. The country came to be known as Vidarbha Lopamudra. He is 'the Seer' of some hymns of the Rgveda. His wife Lopamudra is also mentioned in Rgveda I 179, 4, though Vidarbha is not named therein. The country became well-known in the age of the Brahmanas and the Upanisads. Bhima, who is called Vaidarbha (i.e. the King of Vidarbha), is mentioned in the Aitareya Brahmana (VII, 34) as having received instruction regarding the substitute for soma juice. The Brhadaranyaka Upnisad mentions the sage Kaundinya of Vidarbha. Among those who asked questions about philosophical matters in the Prasnopanisad, there was one named Bhargava from Vidarbha. The Ramayana in the Uttarakanda states the story of king Danda in whose time Vidarbha was devastated by a violent dust-storm. Danda was the son of Iksvaku and grandson of Manu. He ruled over the country between the Vindhya and Saivala mountains from his capital Madhumanta. He led a voluptuous life and once upon a time violated the daughter of the sage Bhargava. The sage, then cursed the king that his whole kingdom would be devastated by a terrible dust-storm. The whole country between Vindhya and Saivala extending over a thousand yojanas was consequently turned into a great forest which since then came to be known as Dandakaranya. It was in this forest that the Sudra sage Sambuka was practising austerities. As this was an irreligious act according to the notions of those days. Rama beheaded him and revived the life of a Brahmana boy who had died prematurely. That the Nagpur region was included in the Dandaka forest is shown by the tradition which states that sambuka was practising austerities on the hill near Ramtek, about 45.062 km (28 miles) from Nagpur. The site is still shown on that hill and is marked by the temple of Dhumresvara. This tradition is at least seven hundred years old, for it is mentioned in the stone inscription of the reign of the Yadava king Ramachandra fixed into the front wall of the garbhagrha of the temple of Laksmana on the hill of Ramtek. The Ramayana, the Mahabharata and the Puranas mention several sacred rivers of Vidarbha such as the Payosni (Purna), Varada (Wardha) and the Vena (Wainganga) and name many holy places situated on their banks. The royal house of Vidarbha was matrimonially connected with several princely families of North India. The Vidarbha princesses Damayanti, Indumati and Rukmini, who married Nala, Aja and Krishna, respectively, are well-known in Indian literature. Several great Sanskrit and Marathi poets from Kalidasa onwards have drawn the themes of their works from their romantic lives.

The region round Nagpur was flourishing in the early centuries of the Christian era, but the name of Nagpur is noticed for the fist time in a record of the tenth century A.D. A copper-plate inscription of the Rastrakuta king Krishna III dated in the Saka yerar 862 (A.D. 940), discovered at Devaji in the Wardha district, records the grant of a village situated in the visaya (district) of Nagpura-Nandivardhana.

Nandivardhana, which was will-known as an ancient capital of the Vakatakas, is now represented by the village Nandardhan, about three miles from Ramtek. Nagpur, which was situated near it, may have marked the original site of the modern town of that name.

Tradition, however, gives the credit for settling the town of Nagpur to the Gond king Bakht Bulanda of Devagad. He is said to have included in the new town twelve hamlets, laid streets and erected a wall for its protection. It is not unlikely that Bakht Bulanda chose to call the new town by the name of Nagpur since it was associated with the place from ancient time.

Coming to historical times, we find that the country was included in the empire of the great Ashoka. The thirteenth rock edict of that great Emperor mentions the Bhojas as the people who follow his religious teachings. The royal family of Bhoja was ruling over Vidarbha in ancient times. An inscription probably issued by the Dharmamahamatra placed by Asoka in charge of Vidarbha, has been found at Devatek in the Chanda district. It records an order promulgated by the Dharmamahamatra interdicting the capture and slaughter of animals. It is dated in the fourteenth regnal year, evidently of Ashoka.

After the overthrow of the Maurya dynasty in circa B.C. 184, the imperial throne in Pataliputra (Patna) was occupied by the Senapati Pusyamitra, the founder of the Sunga dynasty. His son Agnimitra was appointed Viceroy of Malva and ruled from Vidisa, modern Besnagar, a small village near Bhilsa. Vidarbha, which had seceded from the Maurya Empire during the reign of one of the weak successors of Asoka was then ruled by Yajnasena. He imprisoned his cousin Madhavasena, Who was a rival claimant for the throne. The sister of Madhavasena escaped to Malva and got admision as a hand-maid under the name of Malavika to the royal palace. Agnimitra. Who had espoused the cause of Madhavasena and sent an army against the king of Vidarbha, fell in love with Malavika and married her. The Malava army defeated the king of vidarbha and released Madhavasena. Agnimitra then divided the country of Vidarbha between the two cousins, each ruling on one side of the Varada (modern Wardha) Eastern Vidarbha thus comprised Wardha, Nagpur, Bhandara, Chanda, Seoni, Chindvada and Balaghat districts. It was bounded on the east by the country of Daksina Kosala (Chattisgad). From the Mahabharata also we learn that the province of Venakata bordered on that of Kosala. The story of Malavika forms the plot of the play Malavikagnimitra of the great Sanskrit poet Kalidasa.

Kalidasa does not state to what royal family Yajnasena and Madhavasena belonged and these names do not occur anywhere else. Still it is possible to conjecture that they may have been feudatories of the Satavahanas. From the Hathigumpha inscription at Udayagiri near Bhuvanesvar, we learn that Kharavela, the king of Kalinga, who was a contemporary of Pusyamitra, sent an army to the western region not minding Satakarni. The latter evidently belonged to the Satavahana dynasty as the name occurs often in that family. Kharavela's army is said to have penetrated up to the river kanhabenna and struck terror in the hearts of the people of Rsika. The Kanhabenna is the river Kanhan which flows about 10 miles from nagpur. Kharavela's army, therefore, invaded Vidarbha. He knew that as the ruler of Vidarbha was a feudatory of king Satakarni, the latter would rush to his aid when Vidarbha was thus invaded, the people of Rsika (Khandes) which bordered Vidarbha on the west, were naturally terror-striken. No actual engagement seems however to have taken place and the army retreated to Kalinga perhaps at the approach of the Satavahana forces.

The Satavahanas, who are called Andhras in the Puranas, held Vidarbha for four centuries and a half from circa B.C. 200 to A.D. 250. Their earliest inscriptions, however, which record their performance of Vedic sacrifices and manificent gifts to Brahmanas are found in the Poona and Nasik districts. Towards the close of the fist century A.D. they were ousted by the Saka Satraps from Western Maharashtra. They then seem to have found shelter in Vidarbha. No inscriptions of the Satavahanas have indeed been found in Vidarbha, but in one of the Nasik inscriptions Gautamputra Satakarni, who later on exterminated the Sakas and re-occupied Western Maharashtra, is called Benakatakasvami, the lord of Benakataka. No satisfactory explanation of this expression was possible until the discovery of the Tirodi plates of the Vakataka king Pravarasena II. As shown below, these plates record the grant of a village in the Benakata, which must have comprised the territory on both the banks of the Benna or the Wainganga, now included in the Balaghat and Bhandara districts. Gautamiputra was, therefore, ruling over the country of Benakata (or Venakata), before he reconquered Western Maharashtra from the Saka Satrap Nabhapana.

Gautamiputra was a very powerful king whose kingdom extended from the Arabian Sea to the Bay of Bengal and comprised even Malva, Kathiavad and parts of Rajputana in the north. His son Pulumavi was similarly the undisputed master of the whole Deccan. Yajnasri also, a later descendant of the family, retained his old over the whole territory as his inscriptions and coins have been found in the Thana district in the west and the Krishna district in the east. Two hoards of Satavahana coins have been found in Vidarbha, one in the Brahmapuri tahsil of the Chanda district and the other at Tarhala in the Mangul tahsil of the Akila district. The latter hoard, which was discovered in 1939, contains coins of as many as eleven kings. Beginning from Gautamiputra Satakarni. Some of them such as (Gautamiputra) Satakarni, Pulumavi, Sivasri Pulumavi, Yajnasri Satakarni and Vijaya Satakarni are mentioned in the Puranas, while some others such as Kumbha Satakarni, Karna Satkarni and saka Satakarni are not known from any other source. This hoard shows that the Satavahanas retained their hold over Vidarbha to the last.

The Satavahanas were liberal patrons of learning and religion. As stated above, the early kings performed Vedic sacrifices and lavished gifts on the Brahmanas. Gautamiputra, Pulumavi and Yajnasri excavated caves and donated villages to provide for the maintenance, clothing and medicine of Buddhist monks. They also patronised Prakrit literature. The Sattasai. an anthology of 700 Prakrit verses, is, by tradition ascribed to Hala of the Satavahana dynasty.

About A.D. 250 the Satavahanas were supplanted by the Vakatakas in Vidarbha. This dynasty was founded by a Brahmana named Vindhyasakti I, who is mentioned in the Puranas as well as in an inscription in Care XVI at Ajintha. The Puranas mention Vindhyasakti, the founder of the dynasty, as a ruler of Vidisa (modern Bhilsa near Bhopal). His son Pravarasena I ruled over an extensive part of the Deccan. He performed several Vedic sacrifices including four asvamedhas and assumed the title of Samrat (Universal Emperor). According to the Puranas he had his capital at Purika which was situated at the foot of the Rkṣavat or Satpuda mountain. He had four sons among whom his empire was divided after his death. Two of these are known from inscriptions. The eldest son Gautimiputra had predeceased him. His son Rudrasena I held the northern parts of Vidarbha and ruled from Nandivardhana, modern Nandardhan, near Ramtek. He had powerful support of the king Bhava-naga of the Bharasiva dynasty who-ruled at Padmavati near Gwalior who was his maternal grandfather. Rudrasena was a fervent devotee of Mahabhairaya. He has left an inscription incised on the aforementioned slab of stone found at Devatek, which contains as mutilated edict of the Dharmamahamatra of Asoka. It records his construction of a Dharmasthana (temple).

Rudrasena I was followed by his son Parthivisena I, who ruled for a long time and brought peace and contentment to his people, During his reign this branch of the Vakatakas became matrimonially connected with the illustrious Gupta family of north India. Chandragupta II–Vikarmaditya–married his daughter Prabhavatigupta II to Parthivisena I's son, Rudrasena II, Probably Western Ksatrapas. Rudrasena II died soon after accession, leaving behind two sons Divakarasena and Damodarasena alias Pravarasena II. As neither of them had come of age, Prabhavatigupta ruled as regent for the elder son Divakarasena for at least thirteen years. She seems to have been helped in the government of the kingdom by military and civil officers sent by her father Chandragupta II. One of these was the great Sanskrit poet Kalidasa, who, while residing at the Vakataka capital Nandivardhana, must have visited Ramagiri (modern Ramtek), where the theme of his excellent lyric Meghaduta suggested itself to him.

Prabhavatigupta has left us two copper-plate inscriptions. The earlier of them, though discovered in distant Poona, originally belonged to Vidarbha. It was issued from the then Vakataka capital Nandivardhana and records the dowager queen's grant of the village Danguna (modern Hinganghat) to a Brahmana after offering it to the feet of the Bragavat (i.e., Ramachandara) on Karika sukla dvadasi evidently at the time of Parane after observing a fast on the previous day of the Prabodhini Ekadasi Some of the boundary villages can still be traced in the vicinity of Hinganghat.

Divakarasena also seems to have died when quite young. He was succeeded by his brother Damodarasena, who on accession assumed the Pravarasena of his illustrious ancestor. He had a long reign of thirty years and was known for his learning and liberality. More than a dozen land-grants made by him have come to light. One of them which was made at the instance of his mother Prabhavatigupta in the nineteenth regnal year is noteworthy. The plates recording it were issued from the feet of Ramagirisvamin (i.e., God Ramachandra on the hill of Ramagiri) and record the grant which the queen-mother made as on the previous occasion, viz., after observing a fast on the Probodhini Ekadasi.

Pravarasena II founded a new city which the named Pravarapura, where he shifted his capital some time after his eleventh regnal year. Some of his later land-grants were made at the new capital. He built there a magnificent temple of Ramachandra evidently at the instance of his mother who was a devout worshipper of Visnu. Some of the sculptures used to decorate this temple have recently been discovered at Pavnar on the bank of the Dham, 9.656 km. (6 miles) from Wardha, and have thus led to the identification of Pravrapura with Pavnar.

Pravarasena II is the reputed author of the Setubandha, a Prakrit kavya in glorification of Ramachandra. This work has been greatly praised by Sanskrit poets and rhetoricians. According to a tradition recorded by a commentator of this work, it was composed by Kalidasa who ascribed it to Pravarasena. Pravarasena is also known from some Prakrit gathas which were later interpolated in the Sattasai.

Pravarasena II was succeeded by his son Narendrasena, during whose reign Vidarbha was invaded by the Nala king Bhavadatta varman. The latter penetrated as far as the Nagpur district and even occupied Nandivardhana, the erstwhile Vakataka capital. The Rddhapur plates record the grant which Bhavadatta had made while on a pilgrimage to Prayaga. The plates were issued from Nandivardhana which was evidently his capital at the time. In this emergency the Vakatakas has to shift their capital again. They moved it to Padmapura, modern Padampur near Amganv in the Bhandara district. A fragmentary inscription which was proposed to be issued from Padmapur has been discovered at the village of Mohalla in the Durg district.

The Nalas could not retain their hold over Vidarbha for a long time. They were ousted by Narendrasena's son Parthivisena II, who carried the war into the enemy's territory and burnt and devastated their capital Puskari which was situated in the Bastar State. Parthivisena II, taking advantage of the weakening of Gupta power, carried his arms to the north of the Narmada, Inscriptions of his feudatory Vyaghradeva have been found in the former Ajaigad and jaso States.

This elder branch of the Vakataka family came to an end about AD 490. The territory round Nagpur was thereafter included in the dominion of the other or Vatsagulma branch.

The Vatsagulma branch was founded by Sarvasena, an younger son of Pravarasena I. It is also known to have produced some brave and learned princes. Sarvasena. The fonder of this branch, is well-known as the author Prakrit kavya called Harivijaya, which has received unstinted praise from several eminent theoreticians. The last known king of this branch extending from the Arabian Sea to the bay of Bengal and from Malva to the Tungabhadra.

The Vakatakas were patrons of art and literature. In their age the Vaidarbhi riti came to be regarded as the best style of poetry as several excellent works were then produced in Vidarbha. Three of the caves at Ajantha, viz., the two Vihara caves XVI and XVII and the Caitya Cave XIX were excavated and decorated with paintings in the time of Harisena. Several temples of Hindu gods and goddesses were also built. The ruins of one of them have come to light at Pavnar. Others are known from references in copper-plate grants.

The Vakataka disappear from the stage of history about A.D. 550. When their place is taken by the Kalacuris of Mahismati, modern Mahesvar in Central India. They also had a large empire extending from Konkan in the west to Vidarbha in the east and from Malava in the north to the Krishna in the south. The founder of the dynasty was Karsnaraja, whose coins have been found in the Amravati and Betul districts. He was a devout worshipper of Mahesvara (Siva). That Vidarbha was included in Svamiraja dated in the Kalacuri year 322 (A.D. 573). These plates were issued from Nandivardhana which seems to have maintained its importance even after the downfall of the Vakatakas. Svamiraja probably belonged to the Rastrakuta family.

About A.D. 620 the Kalacuri king Buddharaja the grandson of Krishnaraja was defeated by Pulakesin II of the Early Chalukya dynasty, who thereafter became the lord of three Maharashtras comprising 99,000 villages. One of these Maharashtras was undoubtedly Vidarbha. The Rastrakutas, who were previously feudatories of the Kalacuris, transferred their allegiance to the Chalukyas and, like the latter, began to date their records in the Saka era. Two grants of this feudatory Rastrakuta family have been discovered in Vidarbha-one dated Saka 615 was found at Akola and the other dated Saka 631 was discovered at Multai. They give the following genealogy:

Durgaraja

||

Govindaraja

||

Svamikaraja

||

Nannaraja alias Ayuddhsura

(known dates A.D. 693 and 713)

About the middle of the eighth century A.D. the Early Chalukyas were overthrown by the Rastrakutas. No inscriptions of the Early Chalukyas have been found in Vidarbha, but their successors the Rastrakutas have left several records. The earliest of them is the copper-plate inscription of Krishna I discovered at Bhandak and dated in the Saka year 694 (A.D. 772). It records the grant of the village Nagana to a temple of the Sun in Udumbaramanti, modern Rani Amravati in the Yavatmal district. Thereafter several grants of his grandson Govinda III have been found in the Akola and Amravati districts of Vidarbha. The Rastrakutas of Manyakheta and the Kalacuris of Tripuri were matrimonially connected and their relations were generally friendly. But in the reign of Govinda IV, they became strained. The Kakacuri king Yuvarajadeva I espoused the cause of his son-in-low Baddiga-Amoghavarsa III, the uncle of Govinda IV and fought on the bank of the Payosni (Puna) 16.093 km. (10 miles) from Achalpura, between the Kalacuri and Rastrakuta forces, in which the former became victorious. This event is Rajasekhara, which was staged at Triputi in celebration of this victory.

The next Rastrakuta record in Vidarbha is the aforementioned Devali copper-plate grant of the reign of Baddhiga's son Krishna III, which mentions the visaya of Nagapura-Nandi-vardhana.

The Rastrakuta were succeeded by the Later Chalukyas of Kalayani. Only one inscription of this family has been found in Vidarbha. It is the so-called Sitabuldi stone inscription of the time of Vikramaditya VI. From the account of Vinayakrav. Aurangabadkar this record seems to have originally belonged to the Vindhyasana hill at Bhandak. It is dated the Saka year 1008 (A.D. 1087) and registers the grant of some nivartanas of land, for the grazing of cattle, made by a dependant of a feudatory named Dhadibhandaka. Another inscription of Vikramaditya's reign was recently discovered at Dongarganv in the Yavatmal district. It sheds interesting light on the history of the Paramara dynasty. It shows that Jagaddeva, the youngest son of Udayaditya, the brother of Bhoja, left Malva and sought service with Vikramaditya VI, who welcomed him and placed him in charge of some portion of Western Vidarbha. This inscription is dated in the Saka year 1034 (A.D.1112).

Though western Vidarbha was thus occupied by the Later Chalukyas, the Paramaras of Dhar raided and occupied some portion of eastern Vidarbha. A large stone inscription now deposited in the Nagpur Museum, which originally seems to have belonged to Bhandak in the Chanda district, traces the genealogy of the Paramara Prince Naravarman from Vairisimha. It is dated in the Vikrama year 1161 corresponding to A.D. 1104-05, and records the grant of two villages to a temple which was probably situated at Bhandak; for some of the places mentioned in it can be identified in its vicinity. Thus Mokhalipataka is probably Mokhar, 80.47 km. (50 miles) west of Bhandak. Vyapura, the name of the mandala in which it was situated, may be represented by Vurganv 48.280 km. (30 miles) from Mokhar. After the downfall of the Vakatakas, there was no imperial family ruling in Vidarbha. The centre of political power shifted successively to Mahismati, Badami, Manyakheta and Kalyani. Men of learning who could not get royal patronage in Vidarbha, had to seek it elsewhere. Bhavabhuti, who ranks next to Kalidasa in Sanskrit literature, was a native of Vidarbha. In the prologue of his play Mahaviracharita he tells us that his ancestors live in Padmapura in Vidarbha. As stated above, this place with the village Padampur in the Bhandara district. With the downfall of the eighth century when Bhavabhuti flourished there was no great king ruling in Vidarbha. Bhavabhuti had India, and had to get his plays staged at the fair of Kalapriyanatha (the Sun-God at Kalpi). Later, he obtained royal patronage at the court of Yasovarman of Kanauj. Rajasekhara, another great son of Vidarbha, was probably born at Vatsagulma, (modern Vasim), which he has glorified in his Kavyamimamsa as the pleasure-resort of the god of the god of love. He had his ancestors Akalajalada, Tarala and Surananda has to leave their home country of Vidarbha and to seek patronage at the court of the Balaramayana, the Balabharata and the Karpuramanjiri, were put on the boards at Kanauj under the patronage of the Gurjara Pratiharas. Later, when the glory of the Pratiharas declined as sekhara seems to have returned to Tripuri in the train of the victorious conqueror. There his last play Viddhasalabhanjika was staged in jubilation at the victory of Yuvarajadeva over a confederacy of Southern kings led by Govinda IV in the battle of the Paysoni. Another great poet of Vidrbha who had to go abroad in search of royal patronage is Trivikramabhatt, the author of the Nalacampu, in which he has given us a graphic description of several towns, holy paces and rivers of Vidarbha. He flourished at the court of the Rastrakuta king Indra III and is known to have drafted the two sets of Bagumra plates of that king, dated Saka 816.

In the last quarter of the twelfth century A.D. the Yadavas of Devagiri came into prominence. They had been ruling over Seunadesa in an earlier period as feudatories of the Later Chalukyas, but Bhillama, the son of Mallugi, declared his independence and soon made himself master of the whole territory north of the Krishna. He then founded the city of Devagiri, which the made his capital. His son Jaitrapala killed Rudradeva of the Kakatiya whom he had put into prison. Under Jaitrapala's son Singhana the power of the family greatly increased. He annexed the Kolhapur kingdom after defeating the Silahara king Bhoja in

1212. A.D. The first inscription of the Yadavas found in Vidarbha belongs to the reign of Singhana. It is dated in the Saka year 1133 and records the erection of a torana at Ambadaries of Singhana were won for him by his Senapati Kholesvara who hailed from Vidarbha. He defeated Lakmideva, the ruler of Bhambhagiri (modern Bhamer in Khandes), Paramara of Malva, and devastated the capital of the Hoyasalas. He even pressed as far as Varanasi in the north where he put Ramapala to flight. Kholesvara constructed several temples in Vidarbha and also established agraharas on the blanks of the Payosni and the Varada. The former agrahara is still extant under the name of the village Kholapur in the Amravati district.

Singhana was succeeded by his grandson Krishna, whose inscription has been found in the temple of Khandesvara on a hillock on the outskirts of the village Nandganv in the Amravati district. It is dated in the Saka year 1177 (A.D. 1245-55) and records the donations of some gadyanakas for the offerings of flowers at the temple of Khandesvara. After Karsna's death, the throne was occupied by his brother mahadeva superseding the claims of the former's son Ramachandra. Mahadeva annexed Konkan to his kingdom after defeating Somesvara of the Silahara dynasty. He left the throne to his son Amana, but the latter was soon deposed by Ramachandra, who captured the impregnable fort of Devagiri by means of a coup d'etat. He is the last of the independent Hindu Kings of Devagiri. He won several victories and in a grant of his minister Purusottama he is said to have driven out the Muhammedans from Varanasi and built a golden temple there, which he dedicated to Visnu. A fragmentary inscription of his time is built into the front wall of the temple of Laksmana on the hill at Ramtek. In the first half of it, it describes the exploits of Ramachandra's ancestors from Singhana onwards while in the second half it descrbes the temples, wells and tirthas on and in the vicinity of the hill which it names as Ramagiri. The object of the inscription seems to have been to record the repairs done to the temple of Laksmana by Raghava, the minister of Ramachandra. Another inscription of Ramachandra's reign was found at Lanji in the Balaghat district. It is fragmentary and has not yet been deciphered.

In A.D. 1204 Ala-ud-din Khilji invaded the kingdom of Ramachandra and suddenly appeared before the gates of Devagiri. Ramachandra was taken unawares and could not hold out long. He had to pay a large rasom to the Muslim conqueror. He continued, however, to rule till A.D. 1310 at least; for a copper-plate grant which his minister Purusottama made is dated in the Saka year 1232. He was then defeated and slain by Malik Kafur. Some time thereafter Harapaladeva, the son-in-law of Ramachandra, raised an insurrection and drove away the Muhammedans, but his success was short-lived. The Hindu Kingdom of Devagiri thus came to an end in A.D. 1318.

Like their illustrious predecessors, the Yadavas also extended liberal patronage to art and literature. During their age a peculiar style of architecture called Hemadpanti after Hemadri or Hemadpant, a minister of Mahadeva and Ramachandra, came into vogue. Temples built in this style have been found in all the districts of Vidarbha. In the Nagpur district they exist at Adasa. Ambhora, Bhuganv, Darsevani, Savner, Ramtek and some other palces. Several learned scholars flourished at their court. Among those who hailed from Vidarbha, Hemadri was the foremost. During the reign of Mahadeva he held the post of Srikaranadhipa or Head of the Secretariat. He has appointed Minister and Head of the Elephant Force by Ramachandra. He was as brave as he was learned an liberal. He conquered and annexed to the Yadava kingdom the eastern part of Vidarbha called Jhadimandala, Hemadri is well known as the author of the Chaturvargacintamani comprising five parts, (1) Vratakhanda, (2) Danakhanda, (3) Tirthakhanda, (4) Moksakhanda and (5) Parisesakhanda. Of these the third and fourth Khandas have not yet come to light. Hemadri's work is held in great esterm and has been drawn upon by later writers on Dharmasastra. Hemadri wrote on other subjects as will. He is the author of a commentary on Saunaka's Pranavakalpa and also of a Sraddhakalpa in which he follows Katyayana. His Ayurvedarasayana, a commentary on Vagbhata's Astangahrdaya, and Kaivalyadipika, a gloss of Bopadeva's Muktaphala are also well known.

Hemadri extended liberal patronage to learned men. Among his proteges the most famous was Bopadeva. He was a native of the village Vedapada (modern Bedod) on the bank of the Wardha in the Adilabad district of the former Hyderabad State. Bopadeva is said to have composed ten works on Sanskrit grammar, nin on medicine, one for the determination of the tithis, three on poetics and an equal number for the elucidation of the Bhagavata doctrine. Only eight of these are now extant. The Mugdhabodaha, his work on Sanskrit grammar is very popular in Bengal.

Marathi literature also flourished in the age of the Yadavas. Chakradhara, who propagated the Mahanubhava cult in that age, used Marathi as the medium of his religious teachings. Following his example. Several of his followers composed literary works in Marathi. They are counted among the first works of Marathi literature. Mukundaraja, the author of the vedantic works Vivekasindhu and Paramamrta, And Jnanesvara, the celebrated author of the Bhavarthadipika, a commentary on the Bhagavadgita are the most illustrious writers of that age.

2
Geographical Personality of Vidarbha Region

Vidarbh is located right at the heart of the Indian Union occupying 95,868 Sq. Km. area between 19°05' to 21°47' North latitude and 75°59' to 79°11' East Longitude. Vidarbh shares its boundary with the state of Madhya Pradesh towards the north, Chhattisgarh in the east, Andhra Pradesh in the south and Nasik and Aurangabad administrative division of Maharashtra state in the west. Geographically, Vidarbh lies in the fertile plateau between Melghat in the Satpura Range in the north and Balaghat in the Ajanta Range in the south. This area is also known as *Payanghat*. Rich with bounties of nature Vidarbh consists of the Amravati and Nagpur administrative division of Maharashtra. Amravati division comprises of five districts–Buldanana, Akola, Washim, Yavatmal besides Amravati district. The Nagpur division comprises of six districts–Wardha, Bhandara, Gondia, Chandrapur, Gadchiroli besides Nagpur district. In all, Vidarbh represents eleven districts.

Topography

Barring some hilly parts of Satpura range in the north and Ajanta Range in the south the Vidarbh region is largely a fertile plateau, where the average altitude from sea level varies between 200 to 400 meters. This fertile plateau consists of Akola, Amravati, Washim, Yavamal, Nagpur, Wardha districts. The south-eastern part at the confluence of River Wardha and River Wainganga has elevation between 50 to 100 meters. The districts of Gadchiroli and some part of Chandrapur lies in this region. In the north lies the mighty Satpura range having average elevation between 400 to 550 meters. This is home to rich biodiversity, the only hill station of Vidarbh, Chikhadara and the highest peak of Satpura Range is Vairat, which stands at 553 meters above sea level. Politically Vairatis in Amravati district.

Based on the local topography, the state can be identified into following three distinct zones :

1. Northern Satpura Hilly Region
2. Central Fertile Plateau
3. South-Eastern Wardha-Wainganga Doab

Northern Satpura Hilly Region

Satpura range runs parallel to River Narmada, which originates in central India and falls into Arabian Sea. Thus, almost whole of northern Vidarbh comprising Narnala, Akot, Gavilgargh, Chikhaldara, Melghat, Salbardi, Ramtek, Salikasha, Darekasha has hilly slopes. The major southern flowing rivers of Vidarbh namely, Wardha and Wainganga have their origin in Satpura Range. The soil of this region is mixed type and supports several rich and luxuriant species of flora and fauna. The exotic variety of furniture logs viz. Teak, Ain, Dhawda, Haldu, Sesum etc. are found here in abundant. Besides animals like tiger, tendua, deer, bear, bison, nilgai, black buck, flying squirrel and rare bird species have their habitat in this region.

Central Fertile Plateau

The soil of central fertile plateau is typically black in colour due to the presence of a mineral named Motmorelonite. This mineral swells a lot while it is wet. But when it dries it contracts and forms deep crack even up to a depth of two meters. Further due to the presence of alkine limestone layer below it, the black soil becomes very fertile. Buldhana, Akola, Washim, Yavatmal, Amravati, Wardha, Nagpur, Gondia and Bhandara forms part of central fertile plateau. This region has a long list of agriculture products. Cotton, Jowar, Wheat, Pulses, Rice are to name a few. In fact, this region was the largest cotton producing belt in the past. Today, many plantation crops like orange, mango and betelnut are grown in plenty here.

South-Eastern Wardha-Wainganga Doab

Both Wardha and Wainganga river have their origin in Satpura Range in Madhya Pradesh. But they make a doab in Chandrpur and Gadchiroli district and finally flow still south in the name of Pranhita to sub merge in River Godavari. Thus, one can find dense forest in this region that houses many tribal people. Many caves made by the early man is found here as a mute witness of the early civilization that flourished in this region. This plain is also dotted with small hillocks adding beauty to this region. Highly contrasting weather phenomena is a part of this region. It also has a number of mining towns that extracts iron, manganese, and coal. It is thus very ideal for stainless steel plants.

Geologically speaking, most parts of Maharashtra is made up of igneous rocks formed by the molten magma from volcanic eruption. Indian geologists term it as 'Deccan Trap'. Basalt is most abundantly found along with other igneous rocks. In the context of Vidarbha we find rocks little different from the basaltic ones, at Nagpur and to its east, towards north of Amravati and Chandrapur area. In the Nagpur region, which includes Wardha, we find pre-'Deccan Trap' rocks like granite, cyst, grice, sandstone quartzite, lime rocks etc. But it is black soil which found almost everywhere in Vidarbh. Mountains, Rivers and Plains decide the geographic personality of any region and make it noticed. Thus, we can say that the geographical personality of Vidarbh centers around Hilly regions of Bhandara and Chandrapur district, the great Nagpur plateau, the basins of River Wainganga, Wardha, Purna, Painganga, Kanhan.

METEOROLOGY

Temperature

The temperature does not remain the same throughout the year in Vidarbha. February to May is the summer season and the temperature rises up to 42°C to 43°C. At times, it might reach a high of 45°C to 47°C. October to January are considered as winter season and the temperature hovers between 12°C to 14°C. This is considered as an ideal time to visit Vidarbha. As we go higher from the sea level, the temperature decreases and the air becomes cooler. The weather in the high ranges of the Satpura is cool even in summer. One can get a feel of chilly hill station at Chikhaldara in winter when the mercury might drop to sub-zero levels. Being very far from the coast there is very less humidity in the air and the weather is generally dry.

Rainfall

The average rainfall in Vidarbh region is 108 cm. It receives almost 87 per cent of the rainfall from the South-west monsoon between June to September. However, it varies as we go from west to east. Chandrapur, Gadchiroli, Bhandara and Gondia districts receive about 150 cm of rainfall. This becomes an ideal climate to cultivate rice. But the plateau area of Amravati, Buldana, Akola, Yavatmal, Nagpur and Wardha receives little less – about 100 cm of rainfall. It is very ideal for cultivation of food crops like jowar, wheat, pulses an fruits like orange.

Drainage and Water Resources

Drainage system plays a pivotal role in shaping the socio-econonic, ecological and even the cultural personality of any region. Two chief river systems that flows in Vidarbh region are Wardha and Wainganga. Some other major river systems that flow partially in Vidarbh are Godavari, Indravati and Tapi. Other main rivers of the region are Penganga, Wunna, Pranhita, Dina, Nibra, Kotri, Bandia, Jam, Kar, Pench, Kanhan, Kolar, Nag, Dham, Pothra, Asoda, Purna, Nalganga, Katepurna, Vishwaganga, Gyanganga, Banganga, Pendhi, Uma, Nirguna, Man, Bagh, Chulband, Pangoli, Chandan, Bawanthari, Morna and Sur. During the summer when temperature is very high most of these river get dried and there are more rivulets with deep pools here and there. However, during the monsoons some of them become very formidable, especially, Wardha, Wainganga, Penganga and Purna.

Both Wardha and Wainganga originate in Satpura region and run almost parallel before they meet at Sironcha tehsil in Gadchiroli district. From here, they flow together by the name Pranhita before they finally meet Godavari. Another chief river Purna rises in Betul district of Madhya Pradesh and flows due west across Akola district into Buldhada district. Its chief tributaries are Pendhi, Uma, Nirguna,

Man and Katepurna. Towards the southwest of the region the Penganga flows along with its tributaries. It maintains its current through out the year and drains Yavatmal and Washim districts. Down further south it finally meets River Wardha.

In the Wainganga basin of the eastern part of Vidarbha are the districts of Bhandara, Gondia, Chandrapur and Gadchiroli. They are well known as 'lake ditricts'. Bhandara itself has as many as 15,000 lakes. The tanks and lakes in this region are very useful for irrigation. Besides the Upper Wardha Project Amravati district and Pench Project in Nagpur division have big reservoirs that feeds the canals for irrigation.

The major irrigation projects in Amravati Division are Upper Wardha, Arunawati, Wan, Jigaon, Khadakpurna, Lower Painganga, Bembla. Similarly, the major irrigation projects in Nagpur division are Gosikhurd Project, Tultuli Project, Dhapewada Lift Irrigation Scheme, Lower Wardha Project, Human Project, Bawanthadi Project, Lower Wunna Project.

Natural Vegetation

It is the rich biodiversity of Vidarbha that makes it a vacationer's paradise. The soil formation, configuration of the ground drainage and the influence of man mainly govern the type of vegetation. The varying geographical conditions have been ideal for growth of variety of plants and animals. Broadly the vegetation can be divided into the following types:

1. Evergreen Forests
2. Deciduous Forests
3. Thorny Scrub Forests.

Evergreen Forests

Found in the regions receiving heavy rainfall these forests are green throughout the year. The hilly areas of eastern Vidarbha namely Gadchiroli, Chandrapur, Gondia, Bhandara have thick evergreen forests with tall trees and creepers. The trees found in this region are mango (Mangifera Indica), Beheda (Terminalia Belerica), Sisum (Dalbergia Latifolia), Jackfruit, jambul (Eugenia Jambolana), Hirada, Bamboo (Dendrocalamus Strictus) etc.

Deciduous Forest

The trees of these forests shed their leaves at the beginning of summer and get new foliage at the beginning of monsoon. Deciduous forests are found in areas receiving moderate rainfall and are in their full bloom in rainy season. The trees found in these forest are Teak (Tectona Grandis), Khair (Acacia Catchu), Banyan, Peepal, Neem, Ain (Terminalia Tomentosa), Sal, Palas (Butea Frondosa), Tamarind, Amla (Emblica Officinilas), Char (Buchanania Lanzan), Tendu (Diospyros Melamoxylon), Mahua (Madhuca Latifolia), Anjan (Hardwickia Binata), Bel (Aegle Marmelos) etc. Deciduous forests cover large tract of hilly tract of Satpura and Melghat and found mixed with evergreen forests of Gadchiroli, Chandrapur, Gondia and Bhandara district.

Thorny Scrub Forests

Thorny scrub forest covers the trees and scrubs that grow even on infertile land receiving less rainfall. These are found in whole of western Vidarbha, especially the Amravati administrative division. Plants of these forests include Aloe, Tarvad, Agave, Bor (Zizyphus Jujuba), Babul (Acacia Arabica), Stunted Grass etc.

Wildlife

A haven for nature lovers–Vidarbha is a home to large number of animal and bird species including the tiger, crocodile, bison, neelgai, wild deer, sambars and rare migratory birds. The government is trying to take adequate steps towards setting up many wildlife parks and sanctuaries to protect these regions. These parks offer splendid opportunities to see a wide variety of wildlife in the spectacular natural setting. Modern amenities such as jeep rides, night safaris, library and audio-visual facilities, comfortable accommodation and efficient transport are also tried to be made available at these parks at a nominal charge. Nature has bestowed its best in wildlife in Vidarbha. Of a total of 5 National Parks, 2 Tiger Projects, 31 Wildlife Sanctuaries in Maharashtra Vidarbha boasts of 4 National Parks, Both the Tiger Projects and 14 Sanctuaries.

The four National Parks in Vidarbha region are Gugamal (Amravati District), Navegaon (Gondia District), Pench (Nagpur District) and Tadoba (Chandrapur District).

The fourteen Wildlife Sanctuaries in Vidarbha are:

1. Amba-barva Wildlife Sanctuary, Buldana District
2. Andhari Sanctuary, Chandrapur District
3. Bhamragarh Wildlife Sanctuary, Chandrapur District
4. Bor Wildlife Sanctuary, Wardha District
5. Chaprala Wildlife Sanctuary, Chandrapur District
6. Dnyanganga Sanctuary, Buldana District
7. Katepurna Sanctuary, Akola District
8. Lonar Wildlife Sanctuary, Buldana District – Info to be given
9. Melghat Wildlife Sanctuary, Amravati District
10. Nagzira Wildlife Sanctuary, Bhandara District
11. Narnala Wildlife Sanctuary, Akola District
12. Painganga Sanctuary, Yavatmal District
13. Tipeshwar Wildlife Sanctuary, Yavatmal District
14. Wan Wildlife Sanctuary, Amravati District

A detail information about each national park and wildlife sanctuary is given in the Natural attraction section (see chapter 4).

Mineral Wealth

The Chandrapur, Gadchiroli, Bhandara and Nagpur Districts form the main mineral belt, with coal and manganese as the major minerals and iron ore and limestone as potential wealth.

Iron Ore: Iron Ore is found on a very large scale in Chandrapur, Gadchiroli, Nagpur and Gondia districts. Iron and still are obtained from this mineral.

Manganese: Manganese is found on a large scale in Bhandara and Nagpur districts.This mineral is used in the production of steel.

Limestone: Limestone is found in Yavatmal, Chandrapur and Gadchiroli districts. Limestone is used in the production of cement.

Chromite: Chromite mineral is found in Bhandara. It is used in the production of stainless steel.

Coal: Coal is the most important mineral in Vidarbh region. There are coal mines in Nagpur, Yavatmal and Chandrapur districts.This coal is used in fuel in thermal power plants industries.

Other minerals like mica, china clay, copper, etc. are found on a small scale in the eastern parts of vidarbh.

Agriculture

Jowar: Jowar occupies more area than any other crop in Vidarbha. This crop needs warm weather, black fertile soil and moderate rainfall. We see fields of Jowar stretching far in the basins of the rivers Purna, Wardha, Wainganga Morna. It is produce on larger scale in Akola, Yavatmal, Washim, Wardha, Nagpur, Amravati.

Wheat: Wheat is grown in the rabi season. Wheat is grown in the areas which receives moderate rainfall and on fertile land capable of retaining moisture. The cool winter weather is suitable for wheat. It is cultivated in almost whole of Vidarbha but on a larger scale in Nagpur, Amravati and Wardha.

Rice: Rice needs plenty of rain, hot and humid climate and alluvial soil. In Vidarbh region it grown on a large scale in the Waiganga basin in the districts of Bhandara, Gondia, Chandrapur and Gadchiroli.

Bajra: This crop is grown in the kharif season. It needs warm weather, moderate rainfall and less fertile soil. It is cultivated in Washim districts.

Pulses: Major pulses grown in Vidarbha region are Tur, Moong and gram. The centers of cultivationa are Amravati, Buldhana, Akola and Washim.

Fruits: Oranges from Nagpur are famous all over the country and thus gets the sobriquet of "Orange City of India". The plant bears fruit twice a year – in summer and in winter. Oranges grown in summer are bigger and sweeter than oranges grown in winter. There are large orange orchards in Amravati, Yavatmal and Wardha too.

Other fruits that are grown in small scale are mango, banana, grapes, pomegranate, custard apple, guava, sweet lime, watermelon, smashmelon and different varieties of berries.

Vegetables and Spices: Most vegetables used in Indian household are grown in Vidarbh. Prominent among them are

Onions, beans, brinjals, cabbage and leafy vegetable. Vidarbh is one of the largest producers of chilies and coriander seeds in Maharashtra. Nagpur, Amravati, Gadchiroli, Chandrapur are famous for chillies.

Cash Crops

Cotton: Maharashtra is the largest producer of cotton in India and Vidarbha contribute about 80 per cent of it. Cotton is grown in kharif season and picked when it comes out of the balls. The major producing areas are Yavatmal, Akola, Washim, Amravati, Buldhana, Wardha and Nagpur.

Sugarcane: Jaggery, Sugar and treacle are prepared from sugarcane. It is planted in areas where irrigation facilities are available. The major sugarcane growing area in Vidarbha are Amravati, Buldhana, Yavataml and Wardha.

Oilseeds

Main oilseed varieties grown in Vidarbha are groundnuts, sesame, safflower, javas and sunflower. Javas is grown on a large scale in the Vidarbha region. Sesame is grown in Chandrapur and Wardha districts. The main cooking medium of Vidarbha in particular and Maharashtra in general is groundnut oil. The major groundnut growing area are Amravati, Buldhana and Yavatmal. Apart from these we can find a large area under sunflower cultivation.

POWER RESOURCES

Thermal Electricity

A large amount of steam is needed to produce thermal electricity. Coal is used as fuel for producing steam from water and thus thermal electricity power plants are situated near coalfields. Since the eastern part of Vidarbh is full of coalfields, a number of thermal power plants have been established there. Chief among them are Durgapur near Chandrapur, Khaparkheda and Koradi near Nagpur, and Paras near Akola.

Hydro-Electricity

Generally Hydro-Electricity is generated from the multipurpose projects. Here water is accumulated in large reservoirs and then let out from a height in order to rotate large turbines. This on the other hand produces electricity. In Vidarbh, we have such multipurpose projects at Navegaon Bandh, Bor dharan, sillari (pench), Khindsi, Khekranala etc.

On the other hand, Reliance Energy has more aggressive plans. Its management is waiting for the state government's nod to begin its 3,000 MW gas power project in Vidarbh region of Maharashtra.

ECONOMY

Industries–Small Scale

Nagpur is famous center of handlooms and powerlooms. Besides, Yevale produces *pitambari* and raw silk called *kosha* is produced at Savali, Nagbhid, Andhalgaon and Ekodi in Vidarbh. Bhandara and Gondia are well-known for manufacture of utensils of brass, copper and stainless steel. Due to abundance of tendu leaves there are a number of beedi making industries in Gondia, Bhandara and Nagpur. Many poor families make their living by rolling beedi in these units. Since quantitatively Vidarbh produces a good deal of rice one can find many mills for pounding rice. Nagpur has become a hub of fruit processing industries making canned juice, jam, pickle etc. Now days these units use modern equipment producing with greater efficiency and economy.

Industries–Large Scale

Textile Industry: Cotton is carded to remove the seeds, and the carded cotton is pressed into bales. This is called ginning and pressing. The bales of carded cotton are sent to spinning mills. The carded cotton is spun into yarn on spindles. Cloth is made from this yarn or thread. Since cotton is grown in large quantity in Vidarbh we can find textile mills dotted across the region. Some of the important centers are Nagpur, Badnera, Akola, Wardha, Pulgaon etc.

Sugar Industry: These are concentrated on the basins of river Godavari, Pravara, Mula, Bhima, Nira, Krishna, Panchganga etc. We can find many cooperative sugar factories in Nagpur, Amravati, Akola, Yavatmal, Wardha, and Bhandara districts.

Oilseeds: Vidarbh carries a special place in edible oil map of India. Here oil is extracted mainly from groundnut, safflower, javas, cottonseed and sunflower. There are oil-extracting plants at Akola, Washim districts. In Akola *vanaspati ghee* is made from groundnut oil.

Defence Equipment: There are big ordnance factories at Ambazari near Nagpur, Jawahar Nagar near Bhandara and Bhadravati in Chandrapur district.

Wood and Paper: The sprawling forests of Vdarbh have invited many forest-based industry such as wood and paper. There are sawmills at Amravati, Yavatmal and Chandrapur for cutting trees into logs, planks etc. Bamboo, wood and bagasse is used as raw material for paper industry. Such industries are at Ballarpur, Kanhan near Nagpur and Ashti in Gadchiroli.

Other Industries: Factories manufacturing machines and their spare parts, glass and glass articles are found at the industrial estates of at Nagpur. There are factories for purifying manganese at Tumsar and Kamathi in Nagpur region.

Economic Profile of Vidarbha

Item	*Vidarbha*	*Maharashtra*
1. Area	97,404 sq.km	3,07,713
2. Population (1991) 2003 estimated	17.4 million 20.6 million	708.9 million 97.7 million
3. Urban Population (%)	30.2	38.7
4. SC & Buddha (%)	15.02	11.01
5. ST (%)	14.95	9.3
6. Literacy (%) Literacy (%) Male Literacy (%) Female	64.93 76.19 53.03	64.27 76.56 52.32
7. Sex ratio (per 1000 males)	947	934
8. No. of Districts (including Vidarbha)	11	35
9. No. of Villages Total Inhabitated	15,830 13,622	43,027 22,158

Contd...

Item	*Vidarbha*	*Maharashtra*
10. No. of MLAs	65	280
11. No. of MPs	11	
12. Culturable Area (hectares)	5672	20,077
13. Gross Area Sown	6070	22,158
14. Net Area Sown	5027	17,738
15. All Cereals ('000 tones)	1830	8473
16. All Pulses	566	1196
17. Cotton	726	1753
18. Agr. Pumps Energized	4,43,849	22,09,995
19. Working Factories (1998)	3876	28,874
20. Av. daily workers	1,27,006	12,51,759
21. Towns and Villages electrified 1998	13,540	39,413
22. Electricity Installed		10,704 mw
23. Generation		57,927 million kwh
24. Consumption		51,695

TRANSPORT AND COMMUNICATION

Surface Transport

Transport and communication play a pivotal role in the development of any region, more so, in contemporary era of industrialization, modernization and technological advancement. Through speedy movement of men and material, the effective transport system not only ensures economic prosperity but also provides opportunities for much needed inter and intra-community exchanges. Vidarbha incidentally in among those few Indian regions where road and rail transport is fairly developed. It is well connected with the important administrative, commercial and industrial centres and tourist destinations of the country by surface transport.

Road

Vidarbha can boast of one of the finest road links in the country. Located right at the heart of India it has got road connection to the four corners of the country. The Dhule–Kolkata National Highway No. 6 connects Vidarbha to Mumbai in the west and Kolkata in the east. Similarly, the ambitious North-South corridor project connects Vidarbha to Jammu in the north and Kanyakumari in the south. The same corridor also connects Vidarbha to cities like Chandigarh, Delhi, Agra, Gwalior, Jhansi, Bhopal in the north and Hyderabad, Bangalore, Salem in the south.

Railways

Two main broad gauge lines Delhi–Chennai and Mumbai–Kolkata intersect at Nagpur making it the super railway hub of the country. Being *equidistant from and well connected by super fast trains to all the four metropolitan* is the biggest advantage of Nagpur. Given below is the distance of Nagpur from four metros–

New Delhi–1091 RKM   Howrah–1139 RKM
Chennai–1099 RKM   Mumbai–830 RKM

(*RKM: Railway Kilometre*)

Airways

Nagpur is the sole domestic airport of Vidarbha. Besides state owned Indian Airlines private carriers like Jet Airways, Sahara Airlines also operate their flight to and from Nagpur.

Population and Settlement

The distribution of population in the state reflects interplay of physical, economic and the other obvious factors. According to 2001 census, the total population of the Vidarbha has been 20.6 million with the sex ratio 947 females per thousand males. Among the districts, Nagpur has the largest population (22.25% approx) closely followed by Amravati (15% approx) while Washim has the lowest population (7.8% approx). Vidarbha is truly secular in its population mix. Almost all religions, castes and provinces of India are represented in the population of Vidarbha. Not prone to communal violence, unlike rest of Maharashtra.

Districtwise Population Information

Districts	*Area (Sq.Km.)*	*Population (Census 2001)*	*Male Population (Census 2001)*	*Female Population (Census 2001)*
Akola	5,429	1,629,305	840,883	788,422
Amravati	12,210	2,606,063	1,343,572	1,262,491
Bhandara	3,890	1,135,835	573,481	562,651
Buldhana	9,611	2,226,328	1,144,314	1,082,014
Chandrapur	11,443	2,077,909	1,059,875	1,018,034
Gadchiroli	14,412	969,960	490,809	479,151
Gondia	5,431	1,200,151	598,447	601,704
Nagpur	9,892	4,051,444	2,095,489	1,955,955
Wardha	6,309	1,230,640	635,751	591,889
Washim	5,155	1,019,725	525,806	493,919
Yavatmal	13,582	2,460,482	1,267,117	1,193,365

Population of Vidarbha (Census 2001)

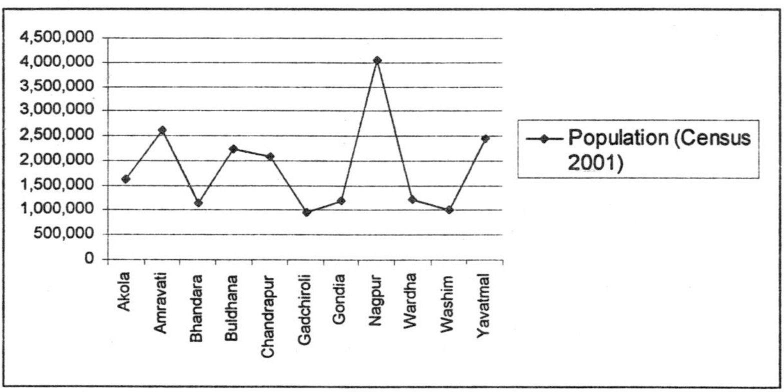

Male-Female Population of Vidarbha (Census 2001)

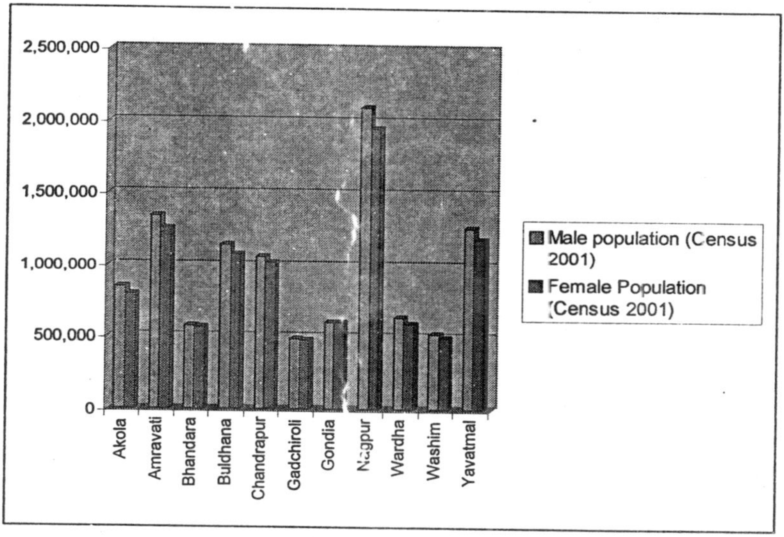

Area (Sq. Km.) of Various Districts of Vidarbha

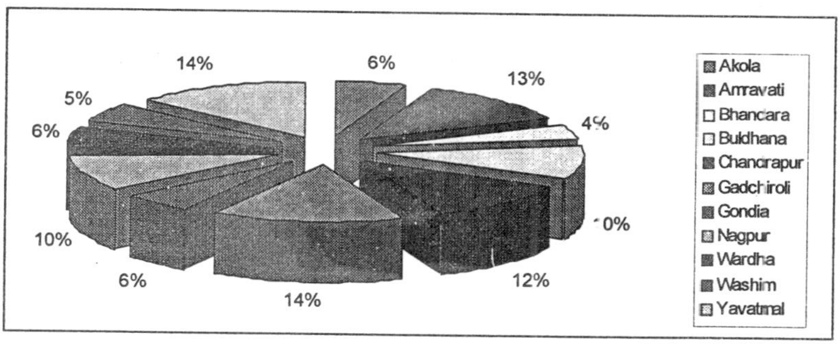

Literacy Rate—Census 2001

Districts	*Total Literacy Rate (In per cent)*	*Male Literacy Rate (In per cent)*	*Female Literacy Rate (In per cent)*
Akola	81.77	89.22	73.82
Amravati	82.96	89.28	76.21
Bhandara	78.69	89.11	68.11

Contd...

Districts	*Total Literacy Rate (In per cent)*	*Male Literacy Rate (In per cent)*	*Female Literacy Rate (In per cent)*
Buldhana	76.14	87.17	64.55
Chandrapur	73.07	83.19	62.56
Gadchiroli	60.29	69.72	50.64
Gondia	78.65	89.54	67.89
Nagpur	84.18	90.25	77.65
Wardha	80.50	87.70	72.80
Washim	74.03	86.01	61.32
Yavatmal	74.06	84.47	63.01

Total Literacy Rate in Vidarbha Region (In Per cent)

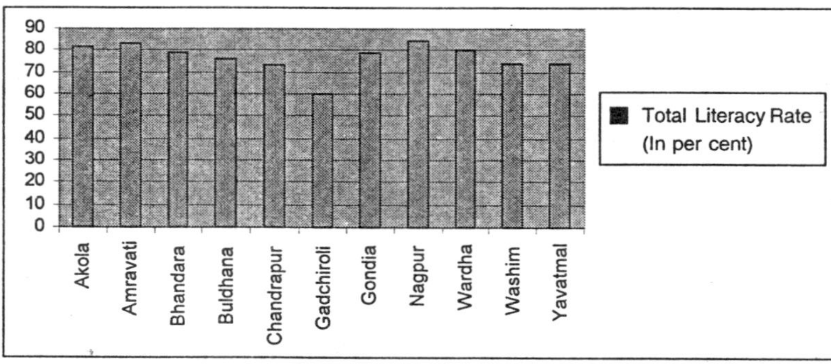

Male Female Literacy Rate in Vidarbha

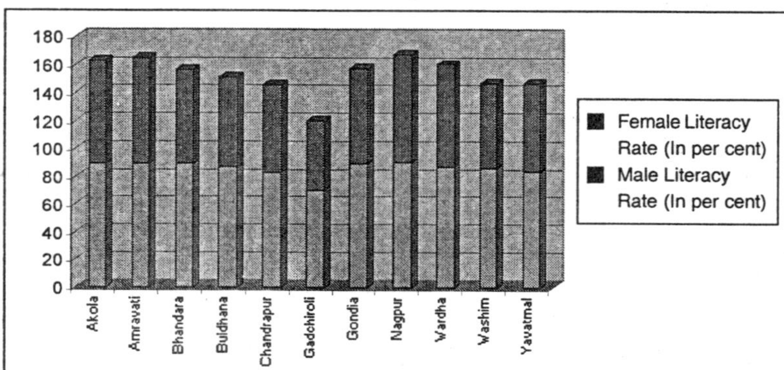

Sex Ratio and Density of Population-Census 2001

Districts	*Sex Ratio (No. of Females per 1000 Male)*	*Density of Population (per sq km)*
Akola	938	300
Amravati	940	213
Bhandara	982	292
Buldhana	946	230
Chandrapur	961	182
Gadchiroli	976	67
Gondia	1005	221
Nagpur	933	413
Wardha	936	195
Washim	939	198
Yavatmal	942	181

Source: www.vidarbhawani.org

Languages

Amongst modern languages English, Marathi and Hindi are spoken in Vidarbha. There are many other tribal languages of the many tribes. The famous Varhadi and Koshti languages spoken in rural Vidarbha and the weaver community respectively are but they are only dialects of Marathi.

Politico-Administrative Divisions of Vidarbha

AKOLA DISTRICT

Location

The district Akola lies between 19°51' North to 21°16' North latitude and 76°38' to 77°44' East longitude in the western parts of the Nagpur division of Maharashtra state and is surrounded by Amravati district in the north, Amravati and yavatmal district in the east, Parbhani and parts of Yavatmal districts in the south and Buldhana district in the west. Total area of the district is 10574 sq.kms. and the district headquarter is located at Akola.

About the District

Akola was named as a district for the first time in 1857. With the reorganization of states in 1956, the district was transferred from Madhya Pradesh to Bombay state. The district forms a part of Maharashtra since 1st May 1960.

The Purna is the chief river of the district. The principal crops grown in the district are cotton, jowar, groundnut, tur, urad, mung, wheat, gram, and sugarcane. There are some large scale manufacturing factories producing textiles and hydrogenated oil. The cotton spinning and weaving mill of Akola town produces both cotton yarn and cloth. Number of small scale establishments like dal-mills, oil presses, confectionary, bidi making, sawmills, soap-making, metal plating and engineering, shoe-making, carpentry, brick-making, pottery, oil-mills etc. There are some important historical forts at Akola, Balapur, Karanja town. Shirpur is a well-known Jain pilgrim center.

Main Languages spoken in the district are Marathi, Hindi, Gujarati, Sindhi and Urdu.

The district at present comprises of 13 tehsils with equal number of community development blocks. It has 10 towns and 1776 villages. While Akola itself is a parliamentary constituency it has six assembly constituencies namely, Khamgaon, Akot, Borgaon manju, Akola, Balapur and Murtijapur.

Climate, Temperature and Rainfall

The climate of the district is characterized by a hot summer and general dryness throughout the year except during the south-west monsoon season. The year may be divided into four seasons. The period from about the middle of November to the end of February constitutes the winter season. The summer season extends from March to June. This is followed by the south-west monsoon season which extends upto the end of September. October and November constitute the post-monsoon season.

During the summers the mean daily maximum temperature of the district is 42.4 degree Celsius while the mean daily minimum temperature is 27.5 degree Celsius. During the winters the mean daily maximum temperature of the district is 29.3 degree Celsius while the mean daily minimum temperature is 11.9 degree Celsius. The average annual rainfall of the district is 846.5 mm.

People and Culture

Akola city is a commercial center and thus the life style there is cosmopolitan in nature. Elsewhere in the district the main occupation of the people is agriculture and their lifestyle is influenced by it. Sakharam Maharaj fair of Loni Budsuk is the important fair of the district.

AMRAVATI DISTRICT

Location

The district is located between 21°46' to 20°32' North latitude and 78°27' to 76°37' East longitude, which essentially indicates that Amravati District is located in the Deccan plateau. Amravati district covers an area of 12626 sq.kms and is situated right in the center of the northern border of the Maharashtra state. It is bounded on the north by Madhya Pradesh, on the east by Nagpur and Wardha district, on the south and south-west by the district of Yavatmal, Akola and Buldhana. The district is divided into 14 Talukas and six sub-divisions.

The District Headquarter is situated at Amravati, which is 150 Kms away from Nagpur, 140 Kms away from Akola and 90 Km from Wardha. Rivers Wardha, Tapi and Puna drain the district.

About the District

The present Amravati district got its existence in the year 1805. During the reorganization of the states in 1956 Amravati district was handed over to Bombay province from Central Province. Later, the district became a part of Maharashtra on 1st May 1960.

Amravati district is well known for Melghat tiger project. It also has the distinction of being the district with largest number of blood donors in Maharashtra. The oranges grown in Amravati have high export value and are sought after in both India and abroad. The other Agriculture Produce in the district are Jowar, Linseed, Tur, Wheat. The Main profession of the people is farming.

Amravati was known as one of the biggest cotton center of India during British rule. It still enjoys the same supremacy though the production of cotton has declined marginally. A train 'Amravati Passenger' that connects Amravati through a narrow guauge line with Badnera junction on the Mumbai-Howrah main line find its mention in The Guiness Book of World Record for being a full fledged passenger train running for shortest distance i.e. 10 Kms.

The district is divided into six Sub-Divisions i.e. Amravati, Chandur (railway), Morshi, Achalpur, Dharni and Daryapur. These six sub divisions are further divided into 14 talukas, 834 Gram Panchayats and 1996 Revenue Villages. The district has three Legislative Assembly Constituencies namely Gadchiroli, Armori and Sironcha. Basically, the district is distributed into 12 talukas and 12 Panchayat Samitis. There are ten Municipalities and one Municipal corporation in the district.

Climate, Temperature and Rainfall

The climate of the district is characterized by a hot summer and general dryness throughout the year except during the south-west monsoon season. The year may be divided into four seasons. The period from about the middle of November to the end of February constitutes the winter season. The summer season extends from March to June. This is followed by the south-west monsoon season which extends upto the end of September. October and November constitute the post-monsoon season.

During the summers the mean daily maximum temperature of the district is 42.1 degree Celsius while the mean daily minimum temperature is 27.2 degree Celsius. During the winters the mean daily maximum temperature of the district is 28.4 degree Celsius while the mean daily minimum temperature is 14.7 degree Celsius. The average annual rainfall of the district is 877.4 mm.

People and Culture

The culture of Amravati along with that of Nagpur said to be the true representation of Vidarbha's culture. Apart from regular Hindu festivals of Holi, diwali, Dussehra, Ganesh Puja the regional festivals like Gudi Padwa, Pola are celebrated with equal fervor. Though in the city people have adopted to modern dress, in the rural areas one can still find men wearing white kurta and cap whereas women wear navari (the nine-yard saree). The food of this region is essentially very hot and spicy.

BHANDARA DISTRICT

Location

Bhandara district is encircled by Balaghat district (M.P.) in north, Gondia in east, Chandrapur, in South, and Nagpur in the West. Hilly region of the northern side consists of Satpuda range, Bhivsen Koka are small hillocks in this range. Gaymukh, Ambagad, these are the prominent hills in northern hilly region.The District of Bhandara has an area of 3965 sq.m. The district is bounded on the N., NE. and E. by lofty hills, inhabited by Gonds and other aboriginal tribes, while the W. and N.W. are comparatively open. Small branches of the Satpura range make their way into the interior of the district.

About the District

More than one-third of the district lies under jungle, which yields gum, medicinal fruit and nuts, edible fruits, lac, honey and the blossoms of the mahua tree (Bassia latifolia), which area eaten by the poorer classes, and used for the manufacture of a kind of spirit. Tigers, panthers, deer wild hogs and other wild animals abound in the forests, and during the rainy season many deaths occur from snake-bites.

Native cloth, brass wares, pot-stone wares, cartwheels, straw and reed baskets, and a small quantity of silk, are manufactured in small quantity. There are 3648 small lakes and tanks in Bhandara district, whence it is called the *Lake District*. They afford ample means of irrigation. The principal crops are rice, wheat, millet, other food-grains, pulse, linseed, and a little super-cane.

Bhandara is the rice bowl of Maharashtra state Chinnor, Dubhraj, Kalikammod, these scented rice varieties from Bhandara district are famous in the State. Natural flora and fauna have enhanced natural beauty and grandeur of the dist.

Climate, Temperature and Rainfall

The climate of the district is characterized by a hot summer and general dryness throughout the year except during the south-west monsoon season. The year may be divided into four seasons. The period from about the middle of November to the end of February constitutes the winter season. The summer season extends from March to June. This is followed by the south-west monsoon season which extends upto the end of September. October and November constitute the post-monsoon season.

People and Culture

The total population of district is 1200151 that includes 598447 males and 601704 females (as per census 2001). Density of Population is 247 per Sq.Km.

The population of schedule tribes is 309822 i.e. 14.70 per cent. The population of schedule caste is 355484 i.e. 16.87 per cent.

The tribals in the district have their own culture. They worships God "Persa Pen" and others. They do the dance "Rela" on auspicious occasions and when new crops come. Rela dance is popular dance among the tribals. The other dance is "Dhol" dance. Holi, Dussehra and Diwali are the main festivals of tribals. The tribal community is resides in the dense forest of District.

The other community peoples are having their own Festival such as Ganpati, Dussehra, Diwali and Holi. In some area of the district, peoples are interested in playing a role in "Natak" or arranges the culture programes "Natak" after Diwali or on Festival days.

Location

The district lies between 20°35' and 21°44' north latitude and 78°15' and 79°40' east longitude at the southern base of satpura

Nagpur District

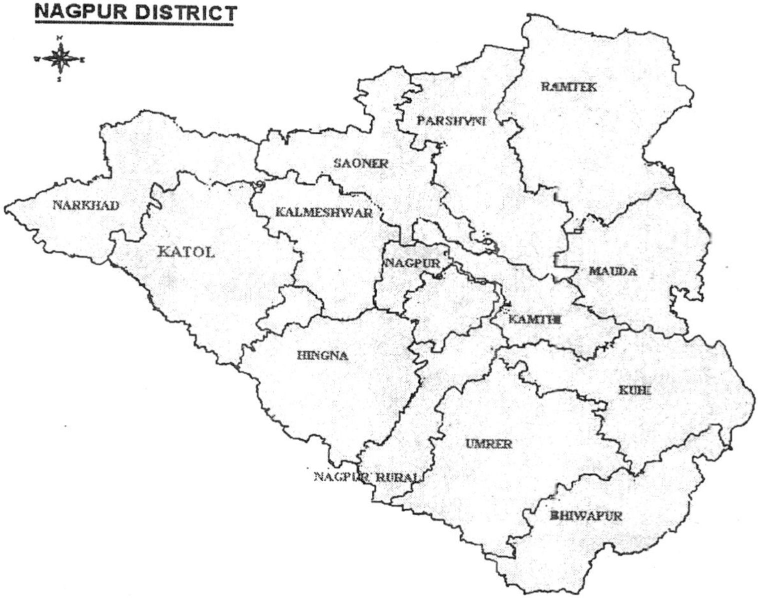

hills. Chhinwara and Seoni districts of Madhya Pradesh fall in its north. Bhandara district flanks it in the east and Chandrapur in the south. Wardha and Amravati districts are contiguous with boundaries in the west. Total area of the district is 9862 sq. kms. The district headquarters is located at Nagpur.

About the District

Nagpur was named as a district for the first time in 1861. With the reorganization of states in 1956, the district was transferred from Madhya Pradesh to Bombay state. The district forms a part of Maharashtra since 1st May 1960.

Wardha and Wainganga are the two main rivers of the district which flow along a part of western and the eastern borders respectively and the drainage of the district is divided between them. Among the chief agricultural produce are jowar, cotton, groundnut, tur, gram, wheat and paddy. But it is the Oranges of Nagpur which makes it famous all over India. Nagpur district is well developed from the view point of commerce and industry with Nagpur city being its hub. Among the large scale industries are cotton textile, saw milling, paper and straw board, ceramics, ferro-manganese, steel re-reeling etc. A unit in Kamptee manufactures safety fuses for blasting gun powder. Small pox and cholera vaccines are manufactures in Vaccine Institute, Nagpur. Apart from that a number important offices of both central and state government are situated here. Some of them are Reserve Bank of India and the Ordnance factory.

Traditional crafts are conducted on household and cottage industries scale and include handloom weaving, oil ghanies, tanning and leather goods manufacture, pottery and bricks, cane and bamboo works, dyeing and printing etc. Nagpur handloom sarees are famous and the silk bordered cloth is exported to various parts of the country. In the recent past the snacks brand name 'Haldiram' of Nagpur has made waves round the country. There are a number of places of tourist interest in and around Nagpur. Chief among them are Adasa, Khapa, Sitabuldi, Ramtek etc. Besides many modem tourist resorts have come up around Nagpur city. Nagpur city plays host to Kalidas Mahotsav every year.

Main Languages spoken in the district are Marathi, Hindi, Gujarati, Punjabi, Sindhi, Telugu and Urdu.

The district at present comprises of 14 tehsils and 13 community development blocks. It has 23 towns and 1878 villages. Nagpur has two parliamentary constituencies. They are Nagpur and Ramtek. It also has 12 assembly constituencies namely, Morshi, Umrer, Katol, Kalmeshwar, Saoner, Ramtek, Kamptee, Nagpur north, Nagpur east, Nagpur south, Nagpur central and Nagpur west. It noteworthy that Nagpur is regarded as the second capital of Maharashtra and the winter session of Maharashtra assembly is held at Nagpur every year.

Climate, Temperature and Rainfall

The climate of the district is characterized by a hot summer and general dryness throughout the year except during the south-west monsoon season. The year may be divided into four seasons. The period from about the middle of November to the end of February constitutes the winter season. The summer season extends from March to June. This is followed by the south-west monsoon season which extends upto the end of September. October and November constitute the post-monsoon season.

During the summers the mean daily maximum temperature of the district is 42.7 degree Celsius while the mean daily minimum temperature is 27 degree Celsius. During the winters the mean daily maximum temperature of the district is 27.7 degree Celsius while the mean daily minimum temperature is 14 degree Celsius. The average annual rainfall of the district is 1161.54 mm.

People and Culture

Nagpur is regarded as mini Mumbai both in terms of its extend and its culture. One can find all modern amenities in the city at hand's reach. People are educated and thus all important fairs and festivals are observed in the district without any discrimination of caste and creed.

WARDHA DISTRICT

Location

The district lies between 20°18' and 21°21' north latitude and 70°30' and 79°15' east longitute. It is bounded in the west and north by Amravati district, in the east by Nagpur district, in the south by Yavatmal district and in the south-east by Chandrapur district. The name Wardha according to local interpretation is a corruption of 'Varaha' or the boar incarnation of Lord Vishnu. The district lies at the foot of the Satpura hills in the Wardha valley. Total area of the district is 6309 sq. kms. The district headquarter is located at Wardha.

About the District

Chandrapur was named as a district for the first time in 1862. With the reorganization of states in 1956, the district was transferred from Madhya Pradesh to Bombay state. The district forms a part of Maharashtra since 1st May 1960.

Important rivers of the district are Wardha and its tributary Wunna. Main crops grown in the district are wheat and jowar. Industries pertaining to general engineering, repairs, fabrication, printing, tanning, manufacture of soap, saw milling, furniture, charkha handlooms, oilcake and agarbatti making are found in the district. The district has an important place in the history because of its association with great leaders like Mahatma Gandhi and Vinobha Bhave. Apart from the ashrams set up by these two leaders Wardha has several pilgim centers for different faiths. Main Languages spoken in the district are Marathi, Hindi and Urdu.

The district at present comprises of 8 tehsils and equal number of community development blocks. It has 6 towns and 1379 villages. While Wardha itself is a parliamentary constituency it has six assembly constituencies namely, Teosa, Chandur, Arvi, Pulgaon, Wardha and Hinganghat.

Climate, Temperature and Rainfall

The climate of the district is characterized by a hot summer and general dryness throughout the year except during the south-west monsoon season. The year may be divided into four seasons. The period from about the middle of November to the end of February constitutes the winter season. The summer season extends from March to June. This is followed by the south-west monsoon season which extends upto the end of September. October and November constitute the post-monsoon season.

During the summers the mean daily maximum temperature of the district is 43 degree Celsius while the mean daily minimum temperature is 27 degree Celsius. During the winters the mean daily maximum temperature of the district is 29 degree Celsius while the mean daily minimum temperature is 13 degree Celsius. The average annual rainfall of the district is 1090.3 mm.

People and Culture

Due to its association with Gandhiji Wardha city is regarded as a dry city. Hindu festivals like Dussehra, shivratri, Holi are dominating in this region. Till date Khadi cloth is spinned by charkha as taught by Gandhiji. There are a number of stupas constructed in the region with the help of Japanese collaboration.

WASHIM DISTRICT

Washim district is surrounded by Buldhana district in the west, Akola district in the north, Yavatmal district in the east and Andhra

Pradesh in the south. Total are of the district is 5155 sq. kms. The district headquarter is located at Washim and is about 80 kms from Akola.

About the District

Washim district was carved out on the 1st July 1998 by the division of erstwhile Akola district. There are six talukas in the district namely, Karanja, Manora, Malegaon, Mangarul Pir, Risod and Washim. According to a belief the astronomers of ancient India drew an imaginary line across the earth and it passed through Washim city. Thus there is a temple named Madhyameshwar dedicated to this Lord Shiva that lies exactly on that imaginary line.

Katepurna, Painganga, Arunavati are the major rivers that drain Washim district. The main crops are Jowar, Mung, Bajra, Wheat, Tur, Orange, Cotton, Gram, and Chilies etc. There are industries pertaining to Cotton-ginning, pressing, oil mill, handloom cloth etc.

Climate, Temperature and Rainfall

The climate of the district is characterized by a hot summer and general dryness throughout the year except during the south-west monsoon season. The year may be divided into four seasons. The period from about the middle of November to the end of February constitutes the winter season. The summer season extends from March to June. This is followed by the south-west monsoon season which extends upto the end of September. October and November constitute the post-monsoon season.

During the summers the mean daily maximum temperature of the district is 42.4 degree Celsius while the mean daily minimum temperature is 27.5 degree Celsius. During the winters the mean daily maximum temperature of the district is 29.3 degree Celsius while the mean daily minimum temperature is 11.9 degree Celsius. The average annual rainfall of the district is 850 mm.

People and Culture

Being a part of the erstwhile Akola district the culture of Washim is not much different from it. Being a new district it is fast running into development. But the people are simple and religious in nature. The fairs and festivals outside the religion are virtually unknown.

YAVATMAL DISTRICT

Location

Yavatmal district lies in the South-Western part of the Wardha Penganga-Wainganga plain. The district lies between 19°26' and 20°42' north latitudes and 77°18' and 79°9' east longitudes. It is surrounded by Amravati and Wardha district to the north. Chandrapur district to the east. Andhra Pradesh State and Nanded district to the south and Parbhani and Akola district.

The district has an area of 13582 sq. km (4.41% of the state) and a population of 2077144 (2.63% of the State). The density of population is 153 persons per km^2 with is less than 257 persons per km^2 for the state as whole.

The district headquarters are located at Yavatmal a town with a population of 108578 as per the 1991 census. It is well connected by roads to the different tahsil headquarters and is also connected to Achalpur by a narrow gauge railway line.

About the District

Yavatmal was named as a district for the first time in 1864. With the reorganization of states in 1956, the district was transferred from Madhya Pradesh to Bombay state. The district forms a part of Maharashtra since 1st May 1960.

The main rivers of the district are the Wardha and Penganga both of which flow skirting the district and forming the district boundaries. Main agriculture produce of the district is Jowar, groundnut, wheat, cotton, oilseeds and tur. Though coal and limestone are found in the district no large scale industries have developed. However small scale industries like handloom, handicrafts, cane and bamboo works, oil ghanis, pottery, leather and tanning, carpentry and smithy etc. are the important industries in the district.

Main languages spoken in the district are Marathi, Hindi, Telugu and Urdu.

The district at present comprises of 12 tehsils and equal number of community development blocks. It has 10 towns and 2108 villages. While Yavatmal itself is a parliamentary constituency it has six assembly constituencies namely, Wani, Ralegaon, Kelapur, Yeotmal, Darwha and Digras.

Climate, Temperature and Rainfall

The climate of the district is characterized by a hot summer and general dryness throughout the year except during the south-west monsoon season. The year may be divided into four seasons. The period from about the middle of November to the end of February constitutes the winter season. The summer season extends from March to June. This is followed by the south-west monsoon season which extends upto the end of September. October and November constitute the post-monsoon season.

During the summers the mean daily maximum temperature of the district is 41.8 degree Celsius while the mean daily minimum temperature is 28.3 degree Celsius. During the winters the mean daily maximum temperature of the district is 28.4 degree Celsius while the mean daily minimum temperature is 15.1 degree Celsius. The average annual rainfall of the district is 991.6 mm.

People and Culture

The district is dominated by forest area and thus the culture is essentially tribal in nature. The major tribes found in this region are Gond and Korku. They have very simple agrarian lifestyle and also resort to cattle farming. Small mining township have developed in the area which is a source of employment for the people. Tribal fair and festivals are celebrated all over the district.

3

Touristic Personality of Vidarbha Region

Personality refers to the totality of somebody's attitudes, interests, behavioural patterns, emotional responses, social roles, and other individual traits that endure over long periods of time. Likewise, the touristic personality refers to the sum total of the tourist resources of a particular destination. The tourist resources can either be man made or natural. Man-made tourist resources are created by inhabitants of that place rather than occurring naturally. It could be either the artifacts like places of worship, museums or the living culture represented by dance, drama, painting, theatre and the like. Whereas natural tourist resources are present in or produced by nature, rather than being artificial or created by people. These may include either the physical resources like the ocean, rivers, mountains, valleys and weather or the biotic resources like flora, fauna and the avi fauna.

In the context of Vidarbha, nature has undoubtedly endowed it with one of the best touristic personalities. It's central location and natural beauty is perhaps unmatched in India. Of the 26 per cent of total forest cover in Maharashtra 21 per cent lies in Vidarbha region. To add to this, it has 3 out of the 4 national parks of Maharashtra. There are a number of excavated sites providing glimpses of the past but are in dilapated condition for the want of consrvation and patronage. With valleys full of velvet mist and majestic trees, an abundance of natural scenery, exciting wildlife, chirupping avi fauna all around, breathtaking waterfalls and a placid lakes, Vidarbh has all that one needs, for an enjoyable holiday. With the promotion of eco-tourism the curret buzzword round the globe, and the unique natural features Vidarbha it can be an instant hit. The hosts of this place are as charming as their surroundings. With their welcoming nature and colourful festivities a visit to Vidarbha becomes an unforgettable experience. For those who would like to actively participate in the activities, can either soak themselves in the perfoming arts of the region or get a direct feel of the primitive yet scientific tribal life. The simplicity of the tribal folks can take one back to thousands of years back making the time stand still. Vidarbha is a part of Gondwana land, which existed even before the Himalayas. Thus it is not surprising to find the fossil remains of the plants and animals of Cabien to Cretacious period. An attempt has been made in this study to enlist the places of tourist interest. Nonetheless, the list is an indicative one and a detailed list would need substantial time and funds.

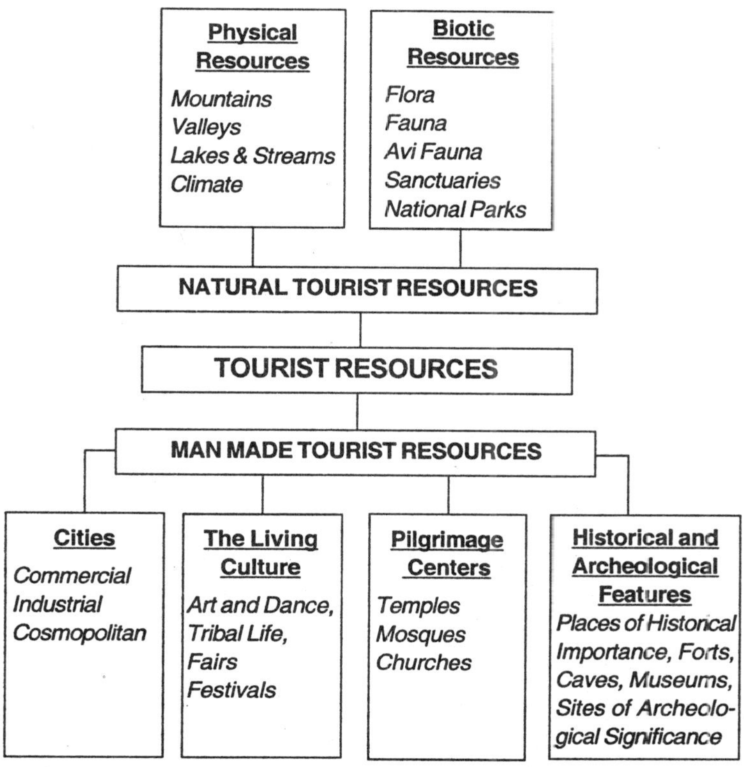

MAN MADE TOURIST ATTRACTIONS IN VARIOUS CITIES OF VIDARBHA

Nagpur

Nagpur popularly known, as Orange capital of India is also the second capital of Maharashtra. The Gond King of Deogad, "Bakht Buland Shah" laid the city's foundation in the year 1702. This city derived its name from the river Nag that flows through it. Nagpur was the capital of Madhya Bharat state (C.P. and Berar) after Indian independence and in 1960, the Marathi majority Vidarbha region was merged with the new state of Maharashtra.

One of well known specialties of Nagpur is the world famous Nagpur orange, the cultivation of which in Vidarbha region of Maharashtra has brought indispensable glory to the region. The orange is cultivated in 80,000 hectares area in Vidarbha with a total production of nearly 5 lakh tons. Nagpur orange in Nagpur district is cultivated in 20,965 hectares area. There is an interesting story how the cultivation of Nagpur orange in this region started. The cultivation of Nagpur orange was tested for the first time as a kitchen garden plant during 1896 by Late Shri. Raghujiraje Bhonsle and observed as a successful venture. Since then, its cultivation attained momentum year after year and by now, it is claimed to be one of the most remunerative potential foreign exchange earning crops of not only this region but also as one of the horticultural crops after mango and banana at national level. An offshoot of orange industry of Nagpur is NOGA (National Orange Growers Association) in Motibagh area of Nagpur which processes and prepares besides Orange juice, 68 other items including jams, squash, marmalades ketchup, sauce, soups and baked beans etc.

Prime Attractions

Ambazari Lake

Lying 6-km west of Nagpur, the Ambazari Lake is the largest and the most beautiful lake in the city. It is one of the most beautiful and well-managed places in the city. The Ambazari garden is a beautiful garden located just beside the lake and the Nagpur Municipal Corporation has developed it as a model garden. It was established in 1958 on an area of 20 acres of land. There are also many items over here to entertain children too.

Balaji Mandir at Seminary

The most popular of Indian deities Shri Balaji, is the presiding deity in this temple situated in the serene and picturesque surroundings of, Nagpur's famed Seminary Hills. This temple also houses the idols of Lord Kartikeya who is believed to be the commanderof the army of Gods.

Sri Poddareshwar Ram Mandir

In the year 1923, this beautiful temple was built with marble and sandstone carving work. The three principle characters of the Indian epic–The Ramayana are the presiding deities.

Sitabuldi Fort

The most important landmark of Nagpur is the historic Sitabuldi Fort, located atop a hill right in the centre of the city. Built in 1857 by a British officer, this is one of the oldest attractions of the city. While passing in front of the Nagpur Railway Station via Kasturchand Park, one can notice this fort, standing on the twin hills of Sitabuldi. The fort now houses the office of the Territorial Army, and is open to the public on National holidays.

Tekdi Ganapathi Temple

Shri Ganesh Tekdi Temple is one of the ancient and most popular temples of Nagpur, located near railway station. The temple is called Tekdi Ganapati as it is constructed on a hill and in Marathi Language a hill is called as a "Tekdi". It is believed to be approximately 250 years old.

It was a ordinary tin shade with a small platform when first built, but it started improving after 1970s, after the Military defense took its possession and in 1965 Late honourable defense Minister Shri Yashwantrao Chavan arranged the possession of the temple and adjoining land to temple trust. The construction of Ganesh temple was started in 1978 and completed in 1984.

Raman Science Center

Raman Science Center is situated opposite to Gandhi Sagar (which is also known as Shukrawari Talao). Although not many people are aware of this center, it is a good place, especially for school children. It has various good working models that demonstrate physical phenomena in an interesting manner.

Museum

This museum has been opened to public after quite a long gap. It houses historical artifacts, which are worth a look.

Seminary Hills

Seminary hills are named after the Seminary of St. Charles, located in a picturesque part of the city, which is quiet and relatively traffic free. There is a Deer Park, which is popular among the kids. Other places which are worth visiting are the Japanese Garden and the shrine of Our Lady of Lourdes, also known as the Grotto.

Maharajbagh

Maharajbagh is one of the oldest attractions of Nagpur. Even though there are relatively few animals here but still this place is considered well for a day's outing, as it is green and pleasant.

Shri Vyankatesh Temple

Shri Vyankatesh Temple is located on Dharaskar Road in Itwari, Nagpur. Respected Chief venerable Swamiji Shri Dharacharyaji brought forward the idea to create Shri Vyankatesh Temple over here. The construction of the temple was started in 1963 and completed in 1968. The statue of the God Vyankatesh is unimaginably beautiful, made of black stone and is decorated with beautiful gold ornaments. Below this main idol there are three festival statues, which are purely made of gold by the skilled artist from Chennai. The main idol of God Vyankatesh had been brought from South India.

Deekshabhoomi

Bharat Ratna Dr B. R. Ambedkar along with thousands of his followers embrassed Buddhism on October 14, 1956 at Deekshabhoomi located at western Nagpur near Ramdaspeth. Since then the site is regarded as a pilgrimage centre for Buddhist. A memorial has since been constructed at the spot. This started with construction of a Bhikshu Niwas in 1968, followed by a P/G degree college and finally a majestic towering monument consisting of replicas of gate of Sanchi Stupa, constructed at a cost of Rs. 6 crores. 5000 Bhikshu can be accomodated in each storey. The diameter and height of the dome is 120 ft. Granites, Marbles and Dholpur Sandstone have been used for the construction of this 4000 sq. ft. hall. The President of India has recently inaugurated this majestic monuments that is a symbol of national integration and secularism and a place of pride for Nagpurians.

Bada Taj Baug

Regarded as one of the four dhaṃs of the four modern era the Dargah has a tomb of Baba Tajuddin Aulia at Nagpur. The other three dhams are of Gajanan Maharaj at Shegaon, Saibaba at Shirdi and Dhuniwale Dadajee at Khandwa (MP).

The tomb attracts tourists from all over India during 'Urs', the annula festival of the Dargah. People from all walks of life from all religions visit and seek blessings at Taj Baug.

The Dragon Palace Temple, Kamptee

Kamptee, satellite township of Nagpur, has recently earned a scintillating identity through the magnificent Dragon palace temple. The unique Buddhist temple with its attractive architecture and landscape was inaugurated on 23 November 1999 by Mother Noriko Ogawa society, Japan on the follow-up by local MLA and minister of state of water and sanitration Ms. Sulekha Kumbhare.

The temple sprawls on 10 acres of land, having a serine and beautiful buddhist prayer centre. A hude idol of Lord Buddha is installed on the first floor of the Meditation hall which is carved out of a Single Sandalwood block. The temple with its characteristic architecture has already received an international award for best concrete structure. The dazzling while walls of the temple signify for peace, purity and divinity. The devotees who assemble there chant 'Nangu-Mayo-Ho-Renge-Kyo' during the meditating hours. The architechtural masterpiece of Nagpur i.e. the Dragon Palace temple is also called 'Lotus Temple' and stands tall amidst sprawling lush green lawns, dotted with flowering plants and laid down in an attractive landscape pattern. The Ogawa society which maintains the temple also looks after allied social activities which include running a mobile hospital, a welfare centre, an orphanage and a school for poor.

Jaadu Mahal, Vishwakarma Nagar

At Vishvakarma Nagar, on Manewada Road is yet another unique place which can truely be called gem of Nagpur. This is a building called Jaadu Mahal (the magic place) which is constructed by famous Magician of Nagpur Late Sunil Bhavsar. This is perhaps the only magic palace in the country with its unique characterisation. In this premises various magic tricks are demonstrated. The Jaadu Mahal remains open even on sundays. Its a treat to visit this gem of Nagpur.

Gangavataran Shiva Statue at Nandanwan

In the premise of Shri Laxmi Narayan temple located in Nandanvan area of east Nagpur, a trust of religious Nagpurian has decided to construct a 51 feet statue of Lord Shiva. The pledged gaint size statue has been designed by sculpture Shri Indrageet Sakharam Tidke of Malakoti distt., Nanded The constructed of this unique statue has already began at the site. Once completed, this will be one of the most magnificiant statues in Vidharbha and perhaps India. It is likely to prove one of major centres of attraction at Nagpur.

Lata Mangeshkar Musical Garden at Surya Nagar

The musical garden is constructed at Surya Nagar, Nagpur under the direction of NIT trustee Jaiprakash Gupta. The sprawling garden besides having having a landscaped garden and lawn, will also have musical fountains, curious architectural sites based on ragas, raganis, and nodes of Indian Classical music which will be operated by musician. There will also be a huge open air theatre sufficient to accommodate about 2500 music loving crowd in the premises where large concerts can be organised. The musical garden when complete, will inspire Children to take up music as their career and will prove to a centre of attraction of Nagpurians.

Few of the other attractions here are the *Bhure Gajanan Devasthan*, a very ancient temple constructed around 250 years back by Bhure Maharaj and *Shri Saibaba Temple.*

Excursions from Nagpur

Totladoh

The Pandit Jawaharlal Nehru National Park is situated in this area. It is surrounded by Satpuda hills providing a pleasant climate. This National Park is best known for animal viewing, bird watching and trekking. There is also situated a hydroelectric project, a joint venture of Government of Maharashtra and Madhya Predesh.

Ramtek

The story goes that Shri Ram tarried here a while with Laxman and Sita. Hence, the name. It was here that the prolific Sanskrit poet Kalidas wrote his epic Maghdootam. Besides the Shri Ram Temple and the Kalidas Memorial, there is Ramgiri hill, Ramsagar lake.This place has been immortalised by the visit of Lord Ram, Sita and Laxman, hence the name Ramtek. The place is also famous as the place where the poet Kalidas composed his epic

"Meghdoot". The main attractions here are the Ram temple which is more than 600 years old, as well as the Jain temple which has some beautiful carvings and sculpture. Ramtek is about 50 kms. from Nagpur.

Nawegaon Bandh

Nawegaon, Vidarbha's most popular forest resort, is the ultimate adventure spot. It is said to have been built by Kolu Patel Kohli in the beginning of the 18th century. There's picturesque lake set in the midst of hill ranges with watch towers that enable you to view wildlife. Make sure you visit the deer park, the Dr. Salim Ali Bird Sanctuary, the three beautiful gardens and the children's park. Almost 60 per cent of the birds species found in Maharashtra have been recorded in Nawegaon. You may see the leopard, sloth bear, gaur, sambar, chital or the langur.

Nagardhan

Nagardhan is an old town and was formerly of considerable importance as it gave its name to the district. It was founded by a Suryawanshi King, but Mr. Hiralal supposes it to have been established by King named Nandvardhan belonging to the Shail Dynasty. There is a fort said to have been built by the Bhonslas with brick walls.

Dhapewada

Dhapewada is situated on the bank of Chandrabhaga river. The town possesses a notable temple of Vithoba, overlooking the river. It was built by Umaji Aba, Diwan to Raja Baji Rao Bhonsla. Dhapewada is being known as Vidarbha's Pandharpur.

Khekranala

Khekranala is a dam site situated in Khapra range forest. This area is palm green and finest natural and fascinating with a bracing climate and healthy environment round the year. The water reservoir is quite and surrounded by thick forest on two side.

Adasa

A small village in the Nagpur District. The village contains fine old temples. In the temple of Ganpati the image consists of a single stone set up so that worshippers may walk around it. On a hill near the village is a temple of Mahadeo with three lingas, which are believed to have come out of the ground by themselves.

Ambakhori

Situated around 60 kms. from Nagpur. It is best in winter, though it tends to be crowded on weekends. It is yet to be developed to its full potential. Waterfalls and a forest are the main attractions.

Pench National Park

Situated around 86 kms. from Nagpur, this National Park is a place good for a day's visit. It is built around the Pench Irrigation project, a joint venture of the Maharashtra and MP Governments. This park is also known as Jawaharlal Nehru Udyan.

Khindsi

Famous mainly for its large and picturesque lake. Boating facilities are also offered. Khindsi is very close to Ramtek, in fact you can combine the two places in a single trip.

Holiday Resorts at Nagpur

Fun N' Food Village, Bazargaon Off Amravati Road

This is the latest addition to the list of Holiday resorts of Nagpur which is setup 30 km. away on Nagpur-Amravati National Highway off Bazargaon. The resort setup in an sprawing area of 300 acres and inaugrated on 21st January 2001 has emmerged as one of the finest amusement parks in the country. The amusement park has international level facilities like Polo trapper, Tora-Tora, Roll N' Roll, Dragon ride Disco and various other interesting facilities where families can enjoy. The village has also setup a beautiful water park having India's largest water slides and wave pool. Here oceanic waves upto a height of 8 feet are artificially created to provide enjoyment to the visitors. There are large scale action reverters also.

This picturesque place located in a small forest between two hillocks, provides a enjoyble surroundings to Nagpurians. Good catering facilites and restaurants are available, however the families are also allowed to carry their pack lunch. A 500 bed dormatory is also started.The management also proposes to start a Tiger safari park where wild animals can be seen roaming freely. A big threatre, water queen, Bumper boards and king wheel is also proposed. While in the final phase facilities for ice skiing and ice park will also being arranged which are available only at three places in the world. The resort is indeed a boon for fun loving Nagpurains.

Ocean Aqua World (Water Park Resort)

This park is located opposite to Ambazari park on Hingna road between two petrol pumps facing the railway line. The water water park is located only 4 km. from Nagpur Octri and is negotiable by city buses upto electronic zone M.I.D.C. from where one can even walk through.

Recently good entertainment and water sports facilities like webpool, slidepool, kids slides, water disco etc. have been arranged besides excellent catering arrangements. Efforts have been made to develop healthy surrounding and green environment where besides picnics, various other types of programmes like membership plan, school picnic plan, get together plan etc.

Kille Kolar

This a newly added restaurant cum resort located on the bank of Kolar river about 15 km. from Nagpur on Chinndwara Road. The restaurant offers a choice sit-down Thali meals and a-la-carte menu. There are also 'chaats' available while watching cultural performance of various talented folk artists drawn from all around the country. Kille Kolar had been modelled on the lines of tradition and folklore of Maharashtra. The entrance itself is constructed as a fort which attracts immediate attention. The deity lord Ganesh welcomes and blesses guests while Chatrapati Shivaji Maharaj provide the rich cultural support. Lush green lawn and environment help in accentuating performance of 'Lavani' and rendering of devotional songs. The traditional 'Khatiyas' invite one for some hours of relaxation. Kille Kolar offers a pure vegeterian restaurant with no scope for alcohol where families can enjoy.

Wakiwoods, Canal Road, Village Waki, Tah. Parseoni, Distt. Nagpur

A creation of Spinner Resorts Private Ltd., the Waki wood is an exquisite picnic spot just 30 km. away from Nagpur to Saoner Road. This private location is enriched by the nature's beauty of a shallow and safe flowing Kolar river, a hillock and mini lake. The wide exhales of the land, which is bordered by a canal on one and river on another. It's tree and it's serene ambiance acquires altoghter new different appearance every season of the year and accord different moods to a visitor and different activities for picnickers. Delicious food is available at reasonable rates at Waki Woods Dhaba.

Starkey Point Resort, Bazargoan, Off Amravati Road

This resort, setup by a local builder Shri K.D. Padole, is located on Nagpur-Amravati Road off Bazargoan, about 35 kms. away. The resort setup, amidst green forest and hilly terrains is on of the popular places for picnicurs, which will be completing 3 years of its existance. The resort offer a swimming pool, restaurant, bar, country club and facilities for horse riding, elephant riding, birds santuary and water park. The beach house restaurant located amidst green hillock, provides place for over 100 guests. The restaurant serves snacks and Chinese food, Continental and Indian taste. An open air theatre having capacity of 400 persons is also available together with facilities for barbeque and kitchen. A wide lawn can be used for cultural programmes, marriage receptions where 600 people can be entertained. There are several slides and rides for amusement of children. 19 rooms are available for those who want to make a night halt.

Ambazari Lake Resort

This is newly renovated lake resort is situated 4 kms. from the city in the south-western part of Nagpur city at its outskits. The lake resort is connected to the city through south Ambazari road as also Amravati road by very good tar-roads. A beautiful rock cut garden has been developed on the slopes of this artificial lake. A small rest house and children park is also developed near by. The Nagpur Corporation has now developed a beautiful amusement park with several modern means of entertainment like Musical fountain, Ghost's House, Magic fountains, Gaint Wheel, Paratrooper, Slum Bob, Water slides, Concorde, Frog ride, Titanic, duck ride, Merry Go Round, etc. Apart from this Appu's Ghar, the picnic spot also offers quite good and well maintained boating and water sports facilities and a food plaza which offers all sorts of food. Sometimes special aeromodelling shows are also organised in this family park. A 4 mtr. high hunter fighter plane of I.A.F. has also been installed here for the children which is the centre of attraction for families.

Amravati

Udumbaravati was the ancient name of today's Amravati. It was due to the presence of ample number of Audumber trees in the region. The name was further abbrevated as Umbravati, Umravati & Amravati. Amaravati meaning "abode of immortals" may be traced with the association of Lord Krishna. The city grown up rapidly at the end of 18th century due to the growth in businesses. It was one of the richest town of the area.

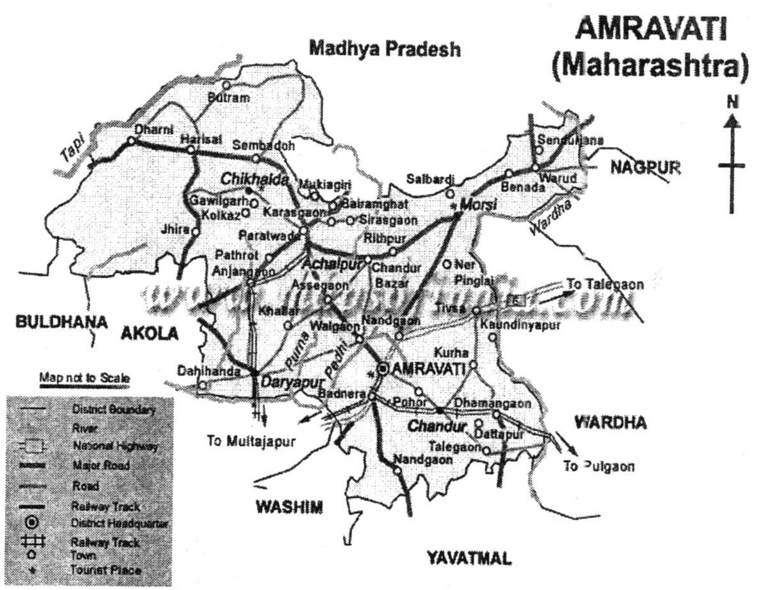

Amravati city is situated 340 m above from the sea level. Pohara and Chirodi hills are in the east of the city. Maltekdi is one of the hills, which gives a bird's eye view of the city. The height of Maltekdi is around 60 m and the statue of great Maratha kind, Shri Shivaji Maharaj is placed on the top of the hill. There are two lakes in the eastern part of the city, namely, Chhatri Talao and Wadali Talao. The city is located in the East Maharashtra on the altitude of 20°56' north and 77°47' east. It is the main centre of west Vidarbha. It is on the Mumbai-Calcutta high way.

History of Amravati

The ancient name of Amravati is "Udumbravati", prakrut form of this is "Umbravati" and "Amravati" is known for many centuries with this name. The mispronunciation form of this is Amravati and now the Amravati is known with the same. It is said that Amravati is named for its ancient Ambadevi temple. The ancient proof of existence of Amravati can get from stone carved inscription on the base of marble statue of God Adinath (Jain God) Rhishabhnath. This shows that, these statues were set up here in 1097. Govind Maha Prabhu visited Amravati in 13th century, at the same time Warhad was under the rule of Deogiri's Hindu King (Yadav). In 14th century, there was famine (drought) in Amravati and people abandoned Amravati and left for Gujarat and Malva. The local people were returned back after several years at Amravati, the result of this was scanty population. In 16th century, Mager Aurangpura (today's, 'Sabanpura') was presented for Jumma Majseed by Badashah Aurangjeb. This reveals that Muslims and Hindus lived together here. In 1722, Chhatrapati Shahoo Maharaj presented Amravati and Badnera to Shri Ranoji Bhosle, by the time Amravati was known as Bhosle ki Amravati. The city was reconstructed and prospered by Ranoji Bhosle after the treaty of Devgaon and Anjangaon Surji and victory over Gavilgad (Fort of Chikhaldara). The British general author Wellesly camped in Amravati, particular place is still recognized as camp, by Amravati people. The Amravati city came in to existence at the end of 18th century. The Amravati was ruled by union state of Nijam and Bosale. They appointed the revenue officer, but defense system was worsted. Gavilgad fort was conquered by Britishers on 15th Dec.' 1803. According to the Deogaon treaty, the Warhad was presented as the token of the friendship to Nijam. The Warhad had Nijams monopoly, thereafter. Near about 1805, Amravati city was attacked by Pendharies. The Sahukars and Marchants of Amravati saved Amravati by giving seven lakhs to the Chittu Pendhari at that time. The Nijam ruled for half century. The people enjoyed British rule instead of cruel Mugals (Nijam). From 1859 to 1871, many government buildings came into existence which were built by the Britishers. Railway station was constructed in 1859, commissioner bungalow in 1860, Small cause court in 1886, (today's S.D.O. OFFICE), the Tahsil office and the Main post office were built in 1871. During this time, the central jail, collector office, Rest house, Cotton market were also built. During 1896, Shri Dadasaheb Khaparde, Shri Ranganath Pant Mudhodker, Sir Moropant Joshi, Shri Pralhad Pant Jog were the leaders in Amravati. The 13th Congress Conference was held at Amravati on 27-29 Dec.' 1897 due to the efforts of these leaders. Shri Lokmanya Tilak and Shri Mahatma Gandhi visited Amravati in 1928. The Muncipal A.V. High School was inaugurated at the hands of Shri Subhash Chandra Bose. At the time of 'Savinay Awagya Andolan', Amravati held the head office of it. On 26th of April 1930, the water was taken from 'Dahihanda' for the famous 'Namak Satyagrah', and Dr. Soman was brought the sea water from Mumbai for the occasion. Around ten thousand people were prepared the salt under the leadership of Shri Vir Vamanrao Joshi.

Prime Attractions

Temples

Ambadevi Temple

Shri Ambadevi Temple is situated at the heart of the city at Gandhi Square. According to the legend it is believed that Shri Krishna abducted Rukmini, when she came to pray at the Amba Devi temple, and married her. The Goddess Amba attracts devotees from all parts of Vidarbha. It is a very old temple and can find it's mention in the old gazetteers. People from all walk of life and from different parts of India visit this temple. The Navaratri Festival, which falls just before Dasara festival, is celebrated by people and the temple authorities with gaiety and Harmony. During these nine days various cultural and religious programs are arranged. Big mela is held on this occasion which is visited by people from all walk of life with same enthusiasm.

Shri Ekviradevi Temple

Shri Ekvira Devi Temple is situated in the vicinity of Amba devi Temple. This Temple is just a few steps away from Amba devi Temple. This is a very old Temple. It was built around the year 1660 by the great son of Amravati Paramhans Shri Janardan Swami. Devi (Godess) is a incarnation of Shakti, during the Navaratri festival the celebration are not separate, everybody who visit Shri Amba Devi also visit Shri Ekvira devi Temple. Ample number of good quality staying facilities are available in various Hotels nearby.

Satidham Temple

Satidham Temple is situated in the heart of the city at Rallies Plot. There are beautiful idols of Lord Krishna-Radha, Lord Ram and Goddess Sita, Lord Ganesh, Lord Shiva and Rani Satiji placed within the temple. Every year a fair is arranged on the occasion of Janmashthami, which is attended by large number of devotees.

Shri Bhakti Dham Temple

Shri Bhakti Dham Temple is situated on Amravati Badnera road where beautiful idols of Lord Krishna and Radha are placed. Shri

Sant Jalaram Bappa idol is also placed and behind this temple a small park for children is maintained.

Shri Ram Temple

Shri Ram Temple, Ziri is situated near Badnera on Amravati - Yavatmal Road. Beautifully carved idols of Lord Ram-Sita is main attraction. Festivities are in the month of April during Shri Ram Navami.

Shri Kondeshwar Temple

Shri Kondeshwar Temple is situated 15 km away from Amravati and 5 Km towards east from Badnera along the hills of pohara forest range. It is a very old Lord Shiva Temple built in carved black stones with "Hemadripant style". Hemadripant was the chief architect of Vijayanagaram Dynasty Kings. His name is now distorted and called as "Hemadpanthi style". This is a very calm place. People visit this place for Shri Shiva Darshana and for peace of mind. Shri Sant Khateshwar Maharaj Samadhi is also situated here. A limited staying facilities are available here.

Shri Maruti Temple

Maruti Temple Chanagapur is situated in the outskirts of Amravati on Amravati-Paratwada road. This is Lord Hanuman Temple. Every Saturday large number of people visit this temple. The festivities are in the month of February-March during Lord Hanuman Jayanti. The season is pleasant during this time and number of people host Vanbhojana here.

Shri Ganesh Temple

Shri Ganesh Temple, Vaygaon is situated 15 Km from Amravati. This Temple is Lord Ganesh Temple build in 15th Century. According to records available and trusties, the foundation stone of this Temple was laid on the same day when Shri Shivaji Maharaja, First Mararta King was ceremoniously took his office.

Shri Aadinath Jain Temple, Bhatkuli

Shri Aadinath Jain Temple is situated 15 km away from Amravati on the banks of the Pedhi River. It is Lord Aadinath Swami Temple. This is one of the important pilgrim for Jain religion. Festivities are in the month of October-November. People from different part of Maharastra take part in it.

Shri Vitthal-Rukhmai Temple

Shri Vitthal-Rukhmai Temple, Koundanyapur is situated 52 km away from Amravati on the western banks of Wardha River. This River is the boundary of Amravati and Wardha Districts. This is very ancient temple. This place is mythologically famous as capital of ancient vidarbha, and a place of in laws of Lord Shri Krishna. The festivities are in the month of October-November. Other Temples are Lord Shiva Temple and Lord Bramha Temple.

Shri Rashtrasant Tukadoji Maharaj Temple

Shri Rashtrasant Tukadoji Maharaj Temple, Gurukunj Mozari, is situated 39 km away from Amravati on Amravati - Nagpur section of national highway 6. This is a holy place graced by the residence of Rashtrasant Tukadoji Maharaj.The Ashrama was instituted by himself. He actively participated in the struggle for freedom movement and also motivated a large number of his follower to take part in it. He was in lime light during "Jungle Satyagraha." After freedom he enlightened the masses against the social evils. He wrote "Gramgeeta" which set the regulations for ideal development of rural persona and development of village itself. Other than his samadhi other temples are his Dhyana Mandir the meditation hall and all religion temple on nearby das tekadi. The festivities are in the month of October-November during his Jayanti.

Shri Sant Gajanan Maharaj Temple

Shri Sant Gajanan Maharaj Temple, Shegaon is situated in Buldhana district of vidarbha region. It is connected by rail route and is a station between Bhusawal and Nagpur. It is situated 150 Km towards west from Amravati. Shri Sant Gajanan Maharaj idol is placed in the beautifully decorated temple. Devotees pour in large number every day from all parts of maharasta and neighbouring states. Ample transportation and staying facilities are available at temple premises mananged by temple authorities. Private hotels are also available. The main festivities are on Shri Ram Navami and Shri Maharaj's mahanirvana day.

Shri Nrusinha Saraswati Temple Karanja

Shri Nrusinha Saraswati Temple Karanja (Lad) is situated 70 Km towards south from Amravati. Along with Amravati (Oomraooti) and Achalpur (Elichapur), Karanja (Lad) was one of the rich city and business centre during 17th century. Shri Nrusinha Saraswati is termed as the incarnation of Lord Dutta Guru in Indian Mythology. He worked for bringing light in the life of poor people. Karanja (Lad) is his birth place. Avery beautiful and attrctive marble idol is placed in the Temple. People from all corner of Maharashtra visit this temple. The Darshana here is the experience of real mental peace. The festivities are in the month of January-February during Shri Nrusinha Saraswati Maharaj's Jayanti. Celebrations last for more than a week.

Vyankatesh Dham Temple

Vyankatesh Dham Temple is situated in the heart of the city, Jaistambh square (This Jaistambh was built on the occasion of independence in 1947). Here idol of Lord Tirupati Balaji is placed. Ample number of good staying facilities are available in various Hotels nearby.

Shri Saibaba Temple, Amravati

Shri Sai Temple, Amravati is situated on Amravati-Badnera Road. A very beautiful idol of Shri Saibaba is placed in the Temple. The idol and internal decoration is just like Shirdi, Saibaba's Karmabhumi. The festivities are in the month of April during Shri Ram Navami. Every Thursday a large number of people from different part of the city visit this temple for Darshana.

Dams and Lakes

Chatri Talao

Chatri Talao is situated towards South-East of Amravati, 1 km from Dasturnagar Square on Malkhed Railway Road. It was built in the year 1888 on a small spring called "Kali Nadi". It is a small reservoir built with the intention, then, to supply drinking water to Amravati City, but now Amravati City gets water from Upper Wardha Dam. A small garden and boating facility is also available.

Wadali Talao

Wadali Talao is situated towards East of Amravati, 3-km from Camp on Chandur Railway Road. It was built for a clean and fresh water supply to Amravati Camp. A small garden with a zoo is also there and usually people come here during weekends. One can also enjoy boating on the Talao. This is one of the best places for kids.

Upper Wardha Dam, Simbhora, Morshi

Upper Wardha Dam is situated at Simbhora, 8 Kms towards the East from Morshi, and 56 Km from Amravati. It is build up on the Wardha River. It is an earthen dam with height of 36 Meters and 7 km length and on the boundary of Amravati and Wardha Districts. It s irrigation capacity is nearly 75000 Hectares of land in these two districts. A tourism center is being developed at this site. It is now named as Nal-Damyanti Sagar.

Shahanoor Dam, Anjangaon Surji

Shahanoor Dam is situated at a site nearly 10 Km towards North-West from Achalpur Tahasil and 85 Km from Amravati. It is build up on the Shahanoor River. It is an earthen dam with 6.9 Km length. It irrigates land of Achalpur and Anjangaon surji Tahsil's. It is situated in the midst of Satpuda Hills and so very picturesque site.(1984-1990).

Kekatpur Talao, Kekatpur

Kekatpur Dam is located towords 6 Km East from the Amravati-Morshi State Highway. It is a kalm place and the waterbodies are such that it is good habitat for birds. In the months of October to January the migratory birds are observed each year. The bird watchers from Amravati and nearby can be regularly seen in the early morning here.

Excursions from Amravati

Melghat: The Melghat Tiger Sanctuary is an area of about 1618 sq. kms of reserved forest straddling the Satpura Range in the Amravati district of Maharashtra. The Satpura hill ranges forms a compact unit of four protected area, spread in two states encompasing roughly an area of 7000 sq. kms. The cluster of three protected areas, the Satpura National Park (524 sq. kms), Bori Wildlife Sanctuary (486 sq. kms) and the Pachmari Wildlife Sanctuary (417 sq. kms) form a unit of 1427 sq. kms. in the state if Madhya Pradesh. Melghat Tiger Reserve in Maharashtra includes the Gugamal National Parklies in the southern tip of Satpuras. The forests are dry, deciduous and mostly of teak. The Melghat Tiger Reserve is one of the last remaining habitats of Indian tiger in Maharashtra.

The Melghat Tiger Reserve was constituted in 1974 and the Directorate of Project Tiger, Melghat started functioning from 22nd Feb. 1974. In view of the ecological, floral and faunal significance of the region, on 5th Sep. 1975, the Melghat Tiger Reserve was designated a sanctuary.

Chikhaldara: The diamond in the necklace of the Satpura ranges and the much loved hill station of Vidarbha. Rich in forests scenic beauty and wild life its a paradise for lovers of nature and wild life.

Early in the 19th century British officer Capt. Robinson, scrambling over the thickly wooded slopes of Satpura hills reached this serene surrounded by forest quite glads and enchanting views at an altitude of 3300 sq. ft., 992 m located deep within the folds of the hills. From then Chikhaldara came into being at a hill station. Chikhaldara environs are full of natural beauty and scenic spots.

Wardha

Wardha, an important district, is placed at a distance of 67 kms from Nagpur. Being associated with Father of The Nation Mahatma Gandhi Wardha is a household name in India. During the freedom movement Wardha was an important center for all political decision makers. But apart from this the not so well known facts about Wardha is that Pauni has been an buzzing city in the ancient India and the recent excavations are testimony to this fact. The peace pagoda set up by Japanese collaboration conducts meditation camps, which are frequented by even the westerners. One of the most intriguing fact about Wardha if that it is a "dry region" viz. alcoholic beverages are discouraged.

Sewagram Ashram

On Gandhiji's final release from prison after his unconditional 21-day self-purification fast in 1933, Gandhiji, who had set out on his famous Dandi march, and pledged not to return to Sabarmati Ashram till independence was achieved, was invited by late Shri Jamnalal Bajaj to stay at Wardha.

Jamnalal Bajaj provided the land of the ashram site and Gandhiji stayed here from 1934 onwards, the premises of the ashram are still maintained in their original state, it is a good place to visit and especially the evening prayers at the ashram. Near the ashram there is a exhibition on the life of Gandhiji.

Paramdham Ashram

Just five miles north of Wardha, is the Ashram of Acharya Vinoba Bhave called the Paramdham Ashram. Young Vinoba longed for self-realisation and left home in search of Brahman. He thought that Bapuji's Ashram would show the light he aspired for and so joined it.

Soon he settled in Paunar, a historic and ancient city of the King Prawarsen, on the banks of the river Dham. After an inner call, he left Paunar and started on an unending Padayatra for Bhoomidan. He regards all the three viz. leaving home, joining

Ashram and leaving for Padayatra are phases towards self-realisation.

The idea of Brahma Vidya was crystallised in 1958 during his morning walks with his associates. His first march from home to Ashram was for individual salvation, but as his thoughts matured, Vinobaji thought that, these cannot and should not be pursued for individual salvation. Real freedom can come to a group mind, working through the group.

While the land at the site of ashram was being excavated some ancient sculptures were unearthed which are about 1500 years old, the sculptures unearthed are on display at the ashram.

Geetai Mandir

This unique temple is a marvelous work of architecture and ingenious design. This temple does not have the traditional ceilings and floorings. The sky is the ceiling, the earth represents the flooring. Inside the temple, there is a small tank of flowing water. The Sun provides light. This way Geetai Mandir seems to be a temple of 'Panchatatva' ie. air, fire, water, earth and sky.

The 'Shlokas' are engraved on the polished stones of Geetai Mandir. The 'Geetai' has 18 sections. Every stone carries one Shloka each of Geetai. The engraved stones are so arranged that the front view of this temple resembles a 'Charkha' and the rear structure resembles the 'cow'.

The temple complex also houses the permanent exhibition on Shri. Jamnalal Bajaj and Aacharya Vinoba Bhave.

Acharya Vinobaji Bhave translated the 'Bhagvada Gita' into Marathi. The book is called 'Geetai' i.e., 'Geeta + Aai' (Mother in the Marathi Language).

Magan Sangrahalaya

Magan Sangrahalaya is the museum for Khadi and Village Industries. It is named after the late Maganlal Gandhi, who helped Mahatmaji to revive the spinning industry in its early stages. Indeed, his premature death was a great loss to the cause of khadi and village industries. It is in the fitness of things that, this museum has been named after him.

The building, though simple in design, has a massive structure with a central hall and two wings. One wing is devoted to khadi and the other to village industries. At the entrance are the images of Yaksha and Yakshi of the Chalukyan type of architecture guardians of this temple devoted to village industries.

Bajajwadi

This is the residence of the late Shri Jamnalal Bajaj who played the host to all the national leaders during the freedom struggle, more specially, at the time of the Congress Working Committee meetings. In the Guest House attached to Bajajwadi, Dr. Rajendra Prasad, Sardar Vallabhbhai Patel, Rajaji, and Maulana Abul Kalam Azad used to stay during their visits to Wardha for meeting Gandhiji. Pandit Jawaharlal Nehru generally stayed in the main Bajajwadi bungalow and occupied the left room on the first floor. Most of the Working Committee meetings were held in this room.

Efforts are afoot to preserve Bajajwadi as it existed during the pre-Independence period. Lunches and dinners were arranged in the back verandah of the main building. All the leaders used to take food in the Indian style, sitting on the floor without tables and chairs. The same style is being maintained even today.

Gandhi Gyan Mandir

This is a public library in front of Bajajwadi. It contains all the books written by Gandhiji and books written on him, in addition to a valuable collection of literature on Economics, Politics and Social Sciences.

The foundation stone of the Gyan Mandir was laid by Dr. Rajendra Prasad in 1950, and it was opened by Pandit Jawaharlal Nehru in 1954.

Laxmi Narayan Mandir

This was the first temple in India which allowed harijans (the people of lower castes) in 1928, the important thing to note is that the temple was made open, without any out side pressure nor with any compulsions.

Rashtra Bhasha Prachar Samiti

This institution was started in 1936 in Wardha under the Presidentship of Dr. Rajendra Prasad, as a result of a resolution of the Hindi Sahitya Sammelan at its Nagpur session.

The Rashtra Bhasha Prachar Samiti conducts Hindi examinations all over India and has published books of learning the national language. It is forefront in promoting Hindi-our national language.

Chandrapur

Chandrapur City, formerly known as Chanda, is located in the south central region of India and lies along a tributary of the Wardha River. It is 150-km away from Nagpur City. Chandrapur is also the district headquarter of the Chandrapur district and it is the largest town in the district with ancient history. Chandrapur means "settlement of the Moon".

The city is surrounded with four historical fort gates and lies particularly in the angle formed by the junction of the Erai and Jharpat rivers and is surrounded by a battlement of over 7 miles in length, which constitutes the most striking example of Gond methods of fortifications that has come down to the present age.

The most attractive feature of the city are the walls that arm the town. A heavy looking crenellated parapet surmounts the walls; they are 10-ft thickness and within run a broad rampart broken down in places. In addition to the walls there are number of temples that attract the tourists.

Viewed from within the city presents a pleasing appearance giving general impression of the space and verdure. The town occupies a site that is underlain by coal bearing rock formation and a number of collieries dot the surface with the waste mounds along the rim of the town.

The ancient history of the district earlier known as Chanda and now Chandrapur is shrouded in mystery. Tradition and legends tell that the name of this place was "Lokapura", which was first changed to "Indupur" and subsequently to Chandrapur. Chandrapur was the capital of the Gond dynasty from 12th to the 18th century.

The Maratha Bhosle of Nagpur later conquered it and it was a part of the British Central Provinces from 1854 until Indian independence in 1947. During the period of the British Raj, Chandrapur came to be called as "Chanda", which was again changed to original name Chadrapur in 1964. Ramala Talav Garden is newly developed place for all ages, especially for kids. Sri Mahakali Temple, Jain Temple at Bhadrawati, and Somnath are famous worship places of this city.

Prime Attractions

Mul

Mul is the largest village in Chandrapur Tehsil, which is picturesquely situated near Mul hills and on the banks of a river, called Huma, which flows in a shallow bed, a mile or two to the east of the village site.

Ballarpur

Ballarpur is a rapidly developing municipal town situated on the Chandrapur-Chennai railway route. It was a royal city in ancient times and signs of its splendour glory are still seen scattered in its environs. Today it is known for its collieries having nearly 2000 million tonnes of coal deposits and large quantities of fine teak and other varieties of timber that are brought from the surrounding forest and sold at Ballarpur.

Bhadrawati or Bhandak

Bhadrawati or Bhandak is a flourishing ancient village in Waroda Tehsil, which is today better known to the general public as a place of Jain religious importance for majestic temple of Parsvanatha than for its historical importance or archaeological remains. The architectural remains in and around the village are of remote antiquity and great interest.

Hemalkasa

Hemalkasa taluka is in Chandrapur district is mostly known for the developmental work by Baba Amte, his wife sadhna Amte and son Prakash Amte. Overwhelmed by the discrimination against leprosy patients. Baba Amte started a residential complex at anandvan in 1973. He named it as Anandvan but laters the tribal of the surroundings area also joined him in his noble work and thus "Anandvan" grew into a happy village. Baba amtes son and his wife who by profession is a doctor, also, used his knowledge for the well-being of the tribals. What makes him special is that he also started a orphanage of animals.started with just one monkey whose mother died during hunting, this unique santury today is a refuge for animals like Tiger, python, lion, dogs, deer, and a lot of birds. Most of thes were either orphans or were injured. Since Dr. Prakash Amte himself treated these animal-patients, all of them enjoy a playful relationship with him. No animal is caged here. The tribals are tought to respect ecology and retrain from hunting. All these efforts by Amte family has been internationally appreciated and a number of national and international awards are testimony to this fact.

Yeotmal

The district has poor heritage of art, architecture, and archaeology. But there are some beautiful temples and other objects of interest. Some of these are at Wani and Moho village in Darwha Tehsil. The temple of Mahadeo in Moho is very beautiful and a large number of visitors visit this temple on every 'Chaitra Amavasya'.

Prime Attractions

Prernastal

On the way to Pusad from Yawatmal lies prernasthal, the memorial of Jawaharlal Darda. Spread across 4 acres of area which shows the shri dardas love for nature. The memorial has a modern style of architecture and is of international standard. There is a huge ampitheatre as soon as we enter prernasthal. It has a sitting capacity of 2000 people and several musical functions are held here. Beyond the ampitheater there is a pool of 200 ft. diameter. there is also a facility of sound and light show. While one side of the ampitheater has flawer garden, the other side has a tall teak forest. Two beams of white light are cast up ward the sky upto 250 mts. This beam of light is on the same lines of the lights at world tred Center in New York. This light can be seen from any wherein yawatmal in night. There is a children park with all amenities like Merry-go round, toy train etc. there is an artificial waterfall near the pool. The different colours of the garden depict different humane qualities, the timing of the premasthal is 6 am to 9 am and 4 pm to 8 pm but the best time to visit is in the evening.

In Yavatmal District Ghanti Baba fair at Digras and Shri Ranganath Swami fair at Wani are the most important fairs. Other important fair is Shir Chintamani fair at Kalamb, Maroti mahraj fair at Ghatanji, Datta Jayanti, at Mahur Jambhora and Mahashivaratri at Wani, Tapona Pusad and Mahagaon. So far trade is concerned, fair are complimentary to the weekly markets. In the fairs, the traders and shop keepers set up temporary stalls. Large quantities of agricultural produce and other articles of daily use are brought for sale. People buy necessary articles in these fairs. Shir Ranganathswami fari is famous for trade in bullock and other cattles.

Forts, old temples and picnic points play an important role in shaping the socio-economic pattern of the district. In Yavatmal district, there are no such historical forts of tourist attraction. A few temples and beautiful picnic spots attract pilgrims and tourists visiting the district.

Datta Mandir located Niranjan Mahur Dhanki and Jambhora, old temple of Narsinha at Anji (Ghatanji), Shir Kehetra Kalamb, Khateshwar Maharaj temple at Jodmoha are important places in the district Hot water springs at Kapeshwar at the bank of Painganga River are the points of attraction for the tourists.

Yavatmal the district headquarters is the biggest city in the district. Ginning Factories, Oil and Pulse Mills and Saw Mills are located in the city. Educational facilities such as Ayurvedic College, polytechnic institution, and college for girls only, Physical Training College are located in the city. Jagat Mandir and Khojochi mosque are important places in the city.

Bhandara

Bhandara is an important trade center of the region. It is considered as the rice bowl of Vidarbha for the quality and quantity of rice produced here. Being a district of thousand lakes one can get variety of fish to eat. The waterbodies also attract a number of migratory birds in winters. It is also an important center for forest produce like honey, *Mahu,* timber and berries etc.

Prime Attractions

Ambagar Fort

This medieval period fort is situated in tumsar taluka and about 13 km away from tumsar in the dist. Fort was constructed by Raja Khan Pathan, the subedar of Bakht Buland Shah, the ruler of Devgadh around 1700 A.D. Later it came under possession of Raja Raghuji Bhosla of Nagpur who used as prison for captives. Later on it had taken over by British.

Andhalgaon

Andhalgaon also known as Andhalgaon or the dark village, is a village of 5,164 inhabitants in 1971 in Bhandara tahsil lying about 16 miles north of Bhandara and connected with Mohali by a good metalled road. It is one of the principal centers in the district having a considerable weaving industry, silk bordered cloths for women being chiefly produced. The *kosa* (silk) cloth for which the district is so well-known has become very costly and hence the demand for it has correspondingly declined. A weekly marked is held on Wednesdays to which some cattle are also brought for sale. Andhalgaon has a primary, an allopathic dispensary, a maternity home, a veterinary aid center, Asarvodaya Sarvodaya Center, and a library. There are also a sub-post office and a police outpost.

Adyar

Adyar, with in 1971 a population of 7,496, is a large village in Bhandara tahsil, situated about 14 miles south of Bhandara on the Pauni road. A number of Gandlis are engaged in weaving silk-bordered saries, cloth and dhotis on handlooms on co-operative basis, the silk-bordered saries being particularly known for their fine texture and quality. Bamboo baskets and matting are also made. At the weekly market held on Sundays household goods, provisions and cattle are put up for sale. In fact Adyar is one of the important cattle markets in the district. The agriculture labourers of this village are known for their skill and knowledge of paddy cultivation and hence are sought after by the agriculturists of the neighbouring villages. The village was previously owned by malguzars but the system of malguzari has since been replaced by the ryotvari system.

Bondgaon

Bondgaon, is a small village of 2.148 inhabitants in 1971 in Sakoli tahsil situated about 13 miles south of Sakoli near the Chulband river. In honors of Gangajumna Devi, who is supposed to dwell in a tank in the Village, a fair is held on Chaitra-Paurnima. The fair lasts for a fortnight, the attendance not exceeding 5,000. On Ashvin Shudha 9 another fair is held. The priest of the temple is much revered and goes about on tour in Chaitra. He is believed to possess the gift of divination and prophecy. Bondgaon has a maternity home an ayurvedic dispensary a veterinary aid center, a post office and facilities for education up to the high school level. For the supply of potable water it depend upon wells.

Brahmi

Brahmi is a small village in Bhandara tahsil lying about 25 miles south of Bhandara. It contains an antique well constructed of long slabs of stone. The local people ascribe its building to the giants or rakshasas. There is a primary school at Brahmi.

Chaundeshwari Devi

This temple is in Mohadi which is about 20 km distance from Bhandara. Many pilgrims visit during Navaratri. This place has been declared as tourism spot of Bhandara.

Chandpur

Chandpur is in Tumsar taluka of Bhandara District. It is situated in hilly ranges and surrounded by dense forest. By constructing a huge wall between two relocks a big reservoir has been created. The reservoir is surrounded by hillocks with dense plantation on remain in portion. One can see fantastic scene beauty by standing on the wall of reservoir. One km. in south of the reservoir is water tank and Chandpur.

Gosikhurd Project/Indirasagar Dam

2,50.800 hectares irrigation potential will be created in Nagpur, Bhandara and Chandrapur districts by this project. Original Administrative approval to the project is accorded for Rs. 372.22 crores on 31st March 1983. 90 per cent of the work has been completed. Rehabilitation-104 villages from Bhandara, 85 villages from Nagpur and 11 villages from Chandrapur are affected by the submergence of Gosikhurd.

Gaimukh

Gaimukh, is a small village of 217 inhabitants in 1971 in Bhandara tahsil 20 miles north of Bhandara and six miles from Ambagad. It is so called because a spring issues from the rocks here, and the name gaimukh or cow's mouth is usually applied to such springs the form of a cow's mouth being sometimes carved out of the rock. There is a cave temple ascribed to the Kuramvars.

Koka

Koka is about 30 km from Bhandara which is covered with dense forest. The trees in this forest are of the age of 100 years. Here the lake is famous for Siberian migrant birds. These birds come in the month of December and return in mid of January.

NATURAL TOURIST ATTRACTIONS OF VIDARBHA

National Parks and Wildlife Sanctuaries

A haven for nature lovers–Vidarbha is a home to large number of animal and bird species. Among the wild animals, the tiger, panther, bison, sambar, chital, nilgai, barking deer, sloth-bear and wild boar are fairly common. The well-known tiger haunts are in the forests of Chandrapur district, Melghat forests of Amarvati district and in the forest of Yavatmal, Nagpur and Bhandara district. The forests of Chandrapur are known as one of the finest tiger beats in the country. Bisons abound in Chandrapur, Nagzira, Pench and Melghat forests. Blackbuck is confined mainly to Yavatmal, Nagpur and Akola. Birds are more varied than animals. The bulbul, shama, cuckoo and parakeet, are either known for their sweet lilt of melody or remarkable mimicry. Among others, are the drongos, babblers, wagtails, paradise flycatchers with their prominent tails, sunbirds, kingfishers, orioles, woodpeckers, bulbuls, hoopoes and the peacock, our national bird, with their gorgeous plumage.

The government is trying to take adequate steps towards setting up many wildlife parks and sanctuaries to protect these regions. These parks offer splendid opportunities to see a wide variety of wildlife in the spectacular natural setting. Modern amenities such as jeep rides, night safaris, library and audio-visual facilities, comfortable accommodation and efficient transport are also available at these parks at a nominal charge.

There are 4 National Parks in Vidarbha region. They are Gugamal (Amravati District), Navegaon (Gondia District), Pench (Nagpur District) and Tadoba (Chandrapur District) National Parks.

1. *Gugamal National Park (Project Tiger Reserve), Melghat*

Melghat Tiger is located in Chikhaldara and Dharni tehsils of Amaravati District in Satpuda hill range.

This tiger reserve of 1676.93 Sq. km. was founded in 1974 with objectives of maintaining viable tiger population and preserving the national heritage for posterity.

There are 750 species of plants in the area. There are 260 species of birds in the published checklist. Serpant eagle, Paradise Flycatchers are commonly seen in the area. The area is rich in wild mammals. Tiger, Leopard, Sloth bear, Wild dog, Jackal, Hyaena, Chausingha, Sambar, Gaur, Barking, deer, Wild boar, Monkeys are commonly seen. Ratel, Pangolin, Cheetal, Mouse deer are rarely seen. There are about 25 types of fishes, many varieties of Butterflies.

2. *Navegaon National Park*

Navegaon, a popular forest resort in the Vidarbha region, the eastern most part of Maharashtra, was built in the 18th century. Navegaon National Park is located in Navegaon, Gondia. Nature here is wreathed in smiles, with the peerless Navegaon Lake spreading its silvery mirror neath the mountains over an expanse of 11 sq. km. The crystal-clear sheet of water presents a scene of sparkling loveliness specially on a moonlit night. The water impounded by the dam at Itiadoh, not far away from Navegaon, would greatly enhance the picturesque beauty around. There is an interesting legend about Navegaon Lake. It is said to have been built by one Kolu Patel Koli at the beginning of the eighteenth century. He is now defined as Kolasur Deo and his shrine is on one of the peaks surrounding the lake. The peaks are known as sat bahini or the ‘seven sisters’. It is believed that these deities helped Kolu in building the lake. On the fringe of the lake is an idol of Hanuman, the deity of strength, whose feet are said to go below the embankment.

Tigers, Panthers, Bisons, Sambars, Nilgais, Chitals, Wild boars, Sloth bears, and Wild dogs are main wild life species in this national park.

The picturesque lake set amidst lush green hills at Navegaon, has a watch-tower beside it. One can get a bird's eye view of the surrounding forest and marvel at the exciting wildlife from the watch-tower. The Dr. Salim Ali Bird Sanctuary, Navegaon is home to almost 60 per cent of the bird species found in entire Maharashtra. Every winter, flocks of beautiful migratory birds visit the lake—a rare treat for the eyes. One can also join the jungle safari and stroll through the beautiful forest, crossing paths with leopards, sloth bears, gaurs, sambars, chitals and langoors. Staying in the unique tree-top house, riding a power or sail boat on the lake, are thrilling pastimes. Nearly 50,000 tourists visits this tourist complex annually. Places of interest around the national park are Nagzira Wildlife Sanctuary (60 km), Itiadoh Dam (20 km), Tibetan Camp at Gothangaon (15 km) and Pratapgad (15 km).

3. *Pench National Park or Pandit Jawaharlal Nehru National Park*

Pandit Jawaharlal Nehru National Park, better known as Pench National Park is located an area of 257.26 sq kms, in Ramtek tehsil of Nagpur. It is enlapped in the Satpura hills, housing a plethora of predators and the florals. Trekking, bird watching and many such activities are best suited to this region. It also houses 25th Tiger Reserve of India. The park nestles in a picturesque setting of hills and dales. Being close to Nagpur city, it bids fair to be a popular tourist center, not only on account of wildlife therein, but also due to scenic beauty of park, to which meandering Pench river lends special charm. nature exhilarates and if it is the art of God one will truly behold it here. There are several low lying gradual hill ranges of satpura fringing this river. In summer the river retains water in pools strewn along its bed, locally known as doh. To the east lies Golia Pahar about 670 meters above the main sea level, which is the highest hill in Nagpur district.

The common animals in this sanctuary are Common Langur, Jackal, Wild dog, Sloth bear, Indian Grey Mongoose, Striped Hyaena, Tiger, Leopard, Jungle Cat, Wild Boar, Spotted Deer, Sambar, Barking Deer, Indian Bison, Nilgai, Chausinga, Large Brown Flying Squirrel, Porcupine, Pangolin.

4. *Tadoba National Park*

Tadoba National Park (116.55 Sq. Kms.)—Andhari wildlife sanctuary (508.85 Sq. Kms.) together form the Tadoba-Andhari Tiger Reserve (625.40 Sq. Kms.). The National Park derives its name from the local tribal God "Taru", whereas the Andhari river flowing through the forests gives the Sanctuary, its name.

Although the major attraction is the Tiger, the large herds of Chital, the stately Sambar, the elusive Barking Deer, the fleet footed Chausinga, the majestic Gaur, the robust Nilgai, the shy Sloth Bear, the whistling Wild dogs, the omnipresent Wild Boar, and the stealthy Leopard make lasting impressions on the visitors to this Reserve.

As the night falls the Small Indian Civet, the Palm Civet, the Ratel, the Flying squirrel make their presence felt. Hyenas, Wild Boars, Spotted Deer, Barking deer, Gaurs, Blue bulls, four horned Antelopes, Indian Pangolins, Porcupines and Common Langoors are main wild animals found in this national park.

Yet another must-see is Tadoba National Park that falls in the Chandrapur district area. Located in the hub of the reserved area, it is believed to be an ideal picnic spot for those who need a desperate break form the routine hassles. Commonly spotted here are tigers, panthers, bisons, sloth bears, hyenas, jackals, wild dogs, blue bulls, sambar, cheetahs, barking deer and a variety of other animals. 205 kms from here is Nagpur. The nearest railhead is Chandrapur, at a distance of 45 kms. Reservation facilities are available with Dy, Conservator of Forest (Wild Life) Chandrapur.

Tadoba National Park is the oldest national park of the State of Maharashtra and since 1993, a Project Tiger Reserve. It derives its name from the local God, "Taru". The legend goes that the village chief "Taru" was killed in an epic fightwith the tiger. He is worshipped by all the local villagers as the deity of "Tadoba"

Tadoba has been referred to as the 'Jewel of Vidarbha'. It has an area of 625 sq.km. This splendid museum of flora and fauna holds more than thousand species of birds, animals, insects and other life forms. Alongwith the main attraction the Tiger, large herds of Chitals, Sambars, Barking Deers, Chausingas, Neel Gais, Sloth Bears, Indian Bisons, Wild Dogs, Wild Boars and Leopards are other inhabitants of this beautiful wildlife sanctuary. Tadoba, a heaven for wildlife enthusiasts is a rich, dry deciduous forest, a great place to walk and enjoy nature. The mesmerising trails of Tadoba could be a treasured experience of a lifetime.This is a large park spread over many acres of lush, green forested land.

Situated 45 kms from Chandrapur, Tadoba is an extremely beautiful jungle park with mixed teak forests around a tranquil lake. Night viewing offers a splendid opportunity to see tigers, leopards, gaurs, nilgais, sambars and chitals. The Tadoba Andhari Tiger Reserve is home to a variety of wild animals. The following wild animals are usually spotted tiger, leopard, leopard cat, Indian wild dog, sloth bear, Hyena, wild boar, spotted deer, barking deer, blue bull, four-horned antelope, Indian pangolin and porcupine. One can also avail of lodging facilities in the park for overnight stay. Around 90,000 people visit the park annually.

There are also 14 Wildlife Sanctuaries in Vidarbha, namely:

1. Amba-barva Wildlife Sanctuary, Buldana District
2. Andhari Sanctuary, Chandrapur District
3. Bhamragarh Wildlife Sanctuary, Chandrapur District
4. Bor Wildlife Sanctuary, Wardha District

5. Chaprala Wildlife Sanctuary, Chandrapur District
6. Dnyanganga Sanctuary, Buldana District
7. Katepurna Sanctuary, Akola District
8. Lonar Wildlife Sanctuary, Buldana District–Info to be given
9. Melghat Wildlife Sanctuary, Amravati District
10. Nagzira Wildlife Sanctuary, Bhandara District
11. Narnala Wildlife Sanctuary, Akola District
12. Painganga Sanctuary, Yavatmal District
13. Tipeshwar Wildlife Sanctuary, Yavatmal District
14. Wan Wildlife Sanctuary, Amravati District

Amba-barva Wildlife Sanctuary, Buldana

The sanctuary is located in Buldana District of Vidarbha region. The sanctuary consist of 2.38 sq.km. private land and 124.73 sq.km. Forest land. The area is hilly and rugged, 823.47 mtr. (MSL) with 500 to 950 mm rainfall. The temperature varies from 35 to 42 degree centigrade. The forest is Tropical Dry Deciduous Forests. Teak, Ain, Salai, Dhawada are the main tree species.The area is ideal habitat of Tiger, Leopard, Sambar, Wildboar, Barking deer, Chousinga (Four horned deer) and birds.

Andhari Sanctuary, Chandrapur

Though a separate administrative unit, this sanctuary is an extended part of Tadoba national park (Project Tiger reserve).

Bhamragarh Wildlife Sanctuary

Bhamragarh Wildlife Sanctuary is home to a variety of wild animals including the following endangered species: the leopard, jungle fowl, wild boar and sloth bear. You can also find the barking deer, blue bull, peacock and flying squirrel among other animals. The land vegetation can be classified as moist deciduous mix forests. The local people in and around the Bhamragarh Wildlife Sanctuary are mostly tribals belonging to the Gond-Madia tribes. They still lead a primitive way of life. The local language is Madia and Gondi. These people are mainly dependent on the forest for their day to day needs such as wood, timber, grass, etc. Other places of interest around the sanctuary are the Hemalkasa Lok Biradari Project run by Dr. Prakash Amte.

Bhor Wildlife Sanctuary

Bhor Sanctuary is to the north of Wardha, in the Hingna range.Wild animals generally spotted are here are the tiger, panther, bison, blue bull, chital, sambar, peacock, barking deer, chinkara, monkey, wild boar, bear, and wild dog.

Chaprala Wildlife Sanctuary

Chaprala Wildlife Sanctuary is home to a variety of wild animals including a few endangered species namely the tiger, leopard, jungle cat, sloth bear and wild dog. There are 131 species of avi-fauna recorded in the protected area of which as many as three bird species are of endangered status. There are two species of reptiles which are of endangered status: the Indian python and common Indian monitar. It is common to spot the following wild animals as well: wild boar, spotted deer, sambar, barking deer, blue bull, jungle cat, jackal, peacock, jungle fowl and flying squirrel. The local people in and around the Chaprala Wildlife Sanctuary are mostly tribals belonging to the Gond community. The local language is Marathi, Telugu, Madia and Gondi. These people are mainly dependent on the forest for their day to day needs such as wood, timber, grass, etc. Other places of other interest around the sanctuary are Prashant Dham at Chaprala, Chaprala Temple and Markanda Temple.

Dnyanganga Sanctuary, Buldana

This protected area is is located mostly in forest area adjoining river Dnyanganga and Buldana tehsil of Buldana district. The terrain is undulating, interspersed with hillocks having gentle slopes. There are two lakes with in santuary.

The protected area is rich in faunal life such as Leopards, sloth bears, barking deers, Sambars, Blue Bulls, spotted deers, hyenas, jungle cats and jackals. The tigers are also sighted in the sanctuary. More then 150 species of birds are recorded in the sanctuary.

Katepurna Sanctuary, Akola

The sanctuary is situated in Akola district in proximity and is mostly the catchments area of Katepurna reservoir.

Forest type: (Southern Tropical dry deciduous forest) Dominant tree species are—Bahada, Dhawada, Moha, Tendu, Khair, Salai, Aola, Teude etc. The detail list of plants includes more than 115 species.

Major wild animals in this sanctuary are Four horned antelope, Black hack, Wolf, Leopard, Hyena, Barking deer, Wild Hoar, Nilgai, Hare, Jungle cat, Monkey etc. Peafowl is common, many species of common birds are seen. Katepurna water reservoir does attract water birds.

Lonar Sanctuary

Being the largest impact crater in the basaltic rock the natural vegetation, flora and fauna of Lonar are unique not only in India but whole world. Therefore, to preserve this uniqueness the area surrounding the Lonar lake has been declared as a wildlife sanctuary.

Melghat – Chikhaldara

Chikhaldara, featured in the epic, the *Mahabharata,* this is the place where Bheema killed the villainous Keechaka in a herculean bout and then threw him into the valley. It thus came to be known as Keechakadara — Chikhaldara is its corruption. But there's more to Chikhaldara. It abounds in wildlife — panthers, sloth bears, sambar, wild boar, and even the rarely seen wild dogs. Close by is the famous Melghat Tiger Project which has 82 tigers.The scenic beauty of Chikhaldara can be enjoyed from Hurricane Point, Prospect Point, and Devi Point. Other interesting excursions include Gavilgad and Narnala Fort, the Pandit Nehru Botanical Gardens, the Tribal Museum and the Semadoh Lake.

Melghat Tiger Reserve

The Melghat Tiger Reserve houses around 120 tigers and is a must-see. Melghat means 'Meeting of the ghats', which is just what the area resembles. Jagged cliffs and steep climbs scar a large tract of unending hills and ravines. At the northern extreme of the Amaravati district on the border of Madhya Pradesh, lies the Melghat Tiger Reserve in the southwestern Satpuda ranges. Melghat Tiger Reserve encompasses an area of 1676 sq.km, at an altitude, ranging from 1024 ft to 3734 ft above sea level. The area has few historic forts and is today the stronghold of the tiger. It was one of the first Project Tiger Reserves in the country. The marvelous expanse of opulent vegetation is home to nearly 720 exotic species of big trees, shrubs, climbers and creepers. Deciduous varieties like Teak and Bamboo are the predominant species of this beautiful forest. Melghat Wildlife Sanctuary is a habitat to many herbivorous and carnivorous species of animals. Blessed by five rivers namely Khandu, Khapra, Sipna, Garga and Dolar, Melghat is an ideal location for study of tribal life, wildlife and vital medicinal herbs. In this rugged forest country and with the right attitude, you could encounter unforgettable experiences everyday. The forest is a part of one of India's most vital tiger breeding habitats.

Nagzira Wildlife Sanctuary

Nagzira has a wildlife sanctuary, gifted with an abundance of wild beasts resting in natural domains, that are a harmonious combination of lush greens and water bodies. The gaur is the star attraction here, along with sambar, deer, and many others from the vicious clan. Nearest railhead is Tiroda 19 kms, nearest airport is Nagpur, 122 kms from here.

Nagzira Wildlife Sanctuary is spread over 153 sq km in Sakoli Taluka of Gondiya District. Nagzira is one of the richest asylums of wildlife and vegetation in Vidarbha. This beautiful jungle was home of elephants in the ancient times. Nagis a sanskrit word for elephant and hence the sanctuary is named as "Nagzira". A picturesque lake is glittering amidst this deciduous forest. Tectona Grandis (Teak) is the predominant variety of this forest having many other trees, herbs and shrubs of medicinal and commercial importance. The Forest department has taken all possible precautions to maintain the seclusion of wildlife. Electric power is not availed here for the same purpose.

Tourists can wander in the woods with the help of guides from the forest department. The jungle trails, named after the rare animals like Bison, Chital, Tiger, keep you anxious and searching for the glimpses of the robust animals of Nagzira.

Many watch towers, water holes, meadows, impression pads are developed here to study the animal life, without disturbing them. The beautiful animals like Tiger, Bison, Sambar, Neelgai, and Chital are living in harmony with the nature. Bird watchers and researchers also visit Nagzira as many exotic species of birds are noticed here.

Nagzira Wildlife Sanctuary is locked in the arms of nature and adorned with a picturesque landscape, luxuriant vegetation and serves as a living outdoor museum to explore and appreciate nature. The sanctuary has a number of fish, approx 34 species of mammals, 166 species of birds, 36 species of reptiles and four species of amphibians. The invertebrate fauna includes, besides a number of insects and ant species, several species of butterflies. Nearly 35,000 tourists visits this sanctuary annually. Wild animals to spot are the tiger, panther, bison, sambar, nilgai, chital, wild boar, sloth bear and wild dog. Other places of interest are Navegaon National Park (50 km), Itiadoh Dam (65 km), Tibetan Camp at Gothangaon (60 km) and Pratapgad (70 km).

Narnala Wildlife Sanctuary, Akola

This sanctuary is located in Akola district of Vidarbha region in continuity to the area of famous Melghat Tiger Reserve in Amravati district. The area of the sanctuary is 12.35 sq.kms. of reserved forests.

The area is hilly and rugged consisting of Tropical Dry Deciduous Forests.Teak, Ain, Tiwas, Salai, Sawar, Erythrina, Lendia, Dhawda, Grewia, Dhaman, Buchanania, Bamboo, Kusum, Sterculia, Moha are the principal plant species in the area. The area is also rich in wild jasmine shrubs. The area is rich habitat of Leopard, Sambar, Barking deer, Wildboar, Serpents, Porcupines and Birds.

Painganga Sanctuary, Yavatmal

The sanctuary is situated on three sides by Painganga river, and its most of the is in Umerkhed tehsil of Yavatmal district. The area is mostly low undulating terrain divided by a wide valley in central region adjoining the district bounded of Nanded and Yavatmal. Predominant forest types and reported are dry teak forest and southern mixed deciduous forests.

Dominant tree species are teak, hald, dhawada, semal salai, ain aola, moha, tendu etc. Plaution works are also done in the past in suitable area.

Tiger, Leopard, Sloth bear, Wild dog, Jackal, Fox, Sambar, Nilgai, Chinkara, Chattel, four horned antelope, Black buck, Wild bear, Hare, Porcupine, Langoor, Monkey.

Common species of birds: Jungle Owl, Partridge, Quails Lapwings, Bee-earths, Chats, Doves, Pigeons, Hopper, Mynahs, Bulbuls, Roller, Parakeets, wagtails, Cuckoos, Koel, Ergot, Robins, Vulture, Kites, Eagles, Harriers, Owls, Egrets, Herons, King fisher, Cormorants, Coot, Teals etc.

Tipeshwar Sanctuary

The animals spotted here are : the black buck, blue bull, chital, sambar, peacock, hare, snake, monkey, wild boar, bear, wild cat, wolf and jackal. Weather : Temperatures are quite pleasant all around the year, although there are three seasons namely summer, winter and the monsoons. Best time to visit is during April and May.

Wan Wildlife Sanctuary, Amravati

This sanctuary is located in Melghat area of Amravati District, and constitutes extension to the Melghat Sanctuary on the south-eastern part. Since the area is part and parcel of Melghat, the hilly rugged terrain possesses Tropical Dry Deciduous forests and the flora and fauna in the area is similar to that of Melghat Tiger Reserve. The area is rich in floral and faunall biodiversity.

The main species of teak, Air, Tiwas, Dhawda, Kusum, Moha and Bamboos.

The area is rich in Tigers, Leopards, Hyena, Wild dogs, Bison, Sambar, Barking deer, Wild boar are major herbivore species.

Lakes and Streams

Khindsey Lake

Khindsey Lake is a gorgeous water body set amidst the green stretch, placed beneath the Ramtek hill. It forms an ideal picnic spot. Eight kms from Ramtek and 60 kms from Nagpur, this lake has a variety of water sports to offer. Fascinating greens and crystal clear waters are set in the backdrop. Regular bus services are available Khindsey lake to Nagpur/Ramtek and vice-versa.

Nawegaon Dam

Nawegaon Dam is termed as Vidarbha's most famous popular forest resort. The resort provides for a hoard of adventure sports to those who expect a thrilling experience to come their way from the place they visit. The dam was built by Kolu Patel Kohli at the start of the 18th century. A picturesque lake adorns the hub of the hill ranges. Watch towers have also been provided to catch the wildlife in action. There exists a deer park nearby called Dr. Salim Ali Bird Sanctuary, along with three fascinating gardens and children's park. Nearest airport is Nagpur at a distance of 142 kms and the nearest rail head is Devalgaon, 1 km on South Eastern Railway. The place is 995 kms from Mumbai and 132 kms from Nagpur. State Transport buses ply from Bhandara, Nagpur and Devalgaon to Nawegaon.

Nawegaon Khairi

Nawegaon Khairi is again a dam site located in Parseoni range forest and forms an ideal picnic retreat. Surrounding the area from three sides is a dense forest. Nearest airport is Nagpur at a distance of 65 kms. The nearest railhead is Nagpur again. State Transport buses ply from Nagpur, Ramtek, Parseoni.

Kanhadevi

Kanhadevi is 30 kms from Nagpur, and the beauty of the place is worth a mention.

Lonar Lake

Lonar Lake is another attraction and takes pride in being the third natural salt-water lake in the world, with a diameter of 1800 meter.

Lonar, the world's largest hyper velocity impact crater in basaltic rock lies in a small town of Buldhana district, 166 km east of Aurangabad. Nearly 50,000 years ago when a meteorite strayed from its celestial path it entered the earth's atmosphere and crashed near Aurangabad. It created a saline lake 433 ft deep and 1.8 km in diameter. This crash had the force of 65-megaton bomb, lighting up the night sky for days after the impact.

Local mythology attributes this phenomenon to a great battle fought when Devi Kamalji slayed a ferocious demon Lonasur at this spot. On the banks of the lake, stand the ruins of beautifully carved Hindu temples. These ancient temples of Lord Shivshankar and Goddess Renuka were constructed in Hemadpanti style.

The soil where the meteor hit and created the third largest crater in the world has become very fertile. The area in and around became lush green and has led to the development of an incredible ecosystem, cradling various species of birds and animals. The animals and birds visible here are migratory Flamingoes, Indian Moorhen, Coot, Dabchick, Langoors, Chinkaras, Peacocks and Gazelles. A section of the society looks at this place as if invaded by extra-terrestrial objects. This fascination for the unknown makes Lonar, one of the few places on earth where we find traces of extra-terrestrial objects.

Khekranala

Khekranala is where a beautiful dam is located. It is situated in the Khapra range forest. The land displays a fine harmony of lush greenery and fascinating surroundings along with healthy environment. Dense foliage blankets the water reservoir. Khekranala is situated at a distance of 55 kms from the main city of Nagpur. Nagpur plays platform to air and rail routes that are closest to Khekranala. State Transport buses ply from Nagpur, Khapra, Saoner.

Kapilaiche Vivar (Chandrapur)

Situated in Korpana taluka of Chandrapur district it is well known for 500 ft. long tunnel. This can be developed as a center of "underground tourism" on the lines of such places in Europe and America.

Sironcha (The Beautiful Border)

Sironcha is a small village on the border of Andhra Pradesh and Maharashtra in Gadhchiroli district. It has the distinction of being the southernmost tip of Vidarbha and thus of Maharashtra also.

Situated on the bank of river pranhita the scenic beauty of this village is really soothing to the eyes. A single glance at the horizon takes one through riots of colors. The red soiled earth, green paddy field, blue-sky tall palm grooves, all at the backdrop of a serpentine river gives one meditative ecstasy. Situated just four kilometers away is the mighty Godavari River, also known as "Dakshin Ganga". A country boat ride from sironcha to the mouth of pranhita where it joins Godavari is worth giving a try. Since Sironcha is the meeting place of Pranhita and Godavari once in every 12 years a sihastha kumbha mela is organized. Devotees from all a cross India gather to take a holy dip here. The cultural life of sironcha is as colourful as its scenery. There is an amalgamation of Telagu and Marathi culture.

Mogarkasa (Nagpur)

Situated on the way to Deola from Nagpur this huge lake is a natural laboratory for botanist and zoologist. The beautiful surroundings have variety of flora and fauna. There are rest houses for tourist accommodation. It is the best place to enjoy sunrise and sunset.

Andhali Sonpur (Gadchiroli)

Nature sometimes exhibits its wonders, which leaves man perplexed. Twenty-five kms from kurkheda taluka in Gadchiroli district there is a village called Andali Sonpur. In the dence forest of this village there are a number of rocks lying here and there. But, only two such rocks, when hit upon with small stones or fingers make a Ting-Ting noise. The wonder is that a hard rock makes a noise of brass or tin. The area surrounding these rocks are called "ting ting" area by the locals. There has been no scientific study on this but it is assumed that due to presence of minerals like manganese and other, the stone could have been an alloy of different minerals. Thus when hit upon produces noise. But such natural phenomenon is rare occurrence and can be promoted to attract tourist from India and abroad. This apart the village also has a historical prominence. Being predominated by tribal, the broken images of tribal gods are found lying here and there. Thus the tribal culture can be preserved to add to the attraction of the area.

Chulbandh

25 Kms from Gondia in Goregaon Tehsil. Rainfed water among the catchment of green hills is the attraction of dam and serene place to relax.

Hazara Fall

50 kms from Gondia in Salekasa Tehsil. A waterfall cascading amidst emerald green vegetation. 1 km from Darekasa railway station. Good camping site.

Itiadoh

85 Kms from Gondia in Morgaon Arjuni Tehsil. The river dam is the source of irrigation for cultivation of Paddy in Gondia, Bhandara and Gadchiroli district. This dam is also known for Katla fish and Prawn culture. Surrounded by hillocks, a veritable feast to onlookers. The Norgying Tibetian settlement, with the Tibetian carpet weaving center is also located near by.

PILGRIMAGE CENTERS OF VIDARBHA

Ramtek

Ramtek...Called so because it was graced by the holy feet of Lord Rama and Sita, his consort. The Ramnavami festival forms the grandeur of the region, but obviously at the Rama Temple that stands proudly atop a hill. The land has been mentioned as Ramgiri, in Meghdootam, one of the fascinating works of Sanskrit poet Kalidas. The Kalidas Smarak, which adorns the hill too, is worth a dekko.

Ramtek is equally a revered site of the Jain community. One can find Nearly 304 cms high, golden coloured idol of Bhagawan Shantinath in the Kayotsarya posture. The history of this tirth is believed to belong to the times of Bhagawan Munisuvrat, the 20th century according to the very ancient Jain puranas or it belongs to the pre-historical times. In the Padmapuran written by

Acharya Raviseno is Vanshagiri, it is stated that Ramchandraji built a number of Jain temples. This vanshagiri is named Ramtek. the idol of Bhagawan Shantinath installed in Ramtek is believed to fulfil heart's desires. On account of exaggerated influence of the idol, this is also called Atishaya Kshetra. Around this temple, there are eight temples. There is also a very splendid and beautiful Manastambh and it is very ancient.

Ramtek is 57 km from Nagpur and is well connected by rail and road to major places in Nagpur. Maharashtra State Transport has daily service with good frequency between Ramtek and Nagpur. The Ramasagar Lake, located close to Ramtek, forms yet another attraction. The main town of Nagpur is distanced by 50 kms from this place. Ramtek is a station that appears on South Central Railway. Regular trains ply between Nagpur and Ramtek.

Adasa

Adasa is a tiny village in the district of Nagpur, a village that houses a plethora of ancient and magnificent temples. The Ganapati temple, that exists here lodges an idol of the Lord, which is a single stone, set up to facilitate easy worship for the devotees. The place lies at a distance of 45 kms from Nagpur and the latter incidentally forms the nearest place housing an airport and a railhead. Access to this place is easy with many buses plying from Nagpur, Kalmeshwar and Saoner. Close to Adasa, is a hill, enlapped in which, is a temple dedicated to Lord Mahadeo with three lingas. The surprising thing about the lingas is that, it is believed.

Ambhora

Situated on the verge of river Vainganga, is a tiny place that houses a well known temple of Chaitanyesvara. Also placed here is the tomb of a Hindu Saint named Har Har Swami. Three main fairs are held here in a year. Ambhora is 74 kms from Nagpur. State Transport buses ply from Nagpur.

Markanda

Markanda, a small parish, located on the left bank of Vainganga river, just seven kms way from charmoshi taluka of Gadhchiroli district is famous as a religious site. The land gets its name from Sage Markandeya. A cluster of temples up of temples exists here housing Shiva Linga which Markandeya is believed to have worshipped. The cluster has an approximate 24 temples... and the architecture strongly resembles that of the Khajuraho temples.what makes it more catchy is the black stone sculpture where as in konark and Khajuraho one finds sandstone sculpture.sadly who built this temple is yet to be known. However according to historian Dr. Mirashi this place was the capital of the Rashtrakuta King Govind iiirdtowards the end of 8th century. This proves that it is older than Khajuraho group of temple. The sculpture twenty four temples around the main Markandeshwar temple depicts Hindu deities like Bramha, Vishnu, Hanuman, Indra, Varuna, Parvati, and different incarnation of the gods and Godesses. There is a series of statues depicting different postures of yogasanas. Due to this beautiful sculptures markandeshwar is regarded as vidarbhas Khajuraho or Dakshin Kashi. During the Hindu month of Shravana a big fair is organized and lakhs of devotees throng this place to pay their obeisance to lord Markandeshwar.The nearest airport is Nagpur at a distance of 177 kms. The nearest railhead is Chandrapur, 91 kms from here.

Dhapewada

Dhapewada, lies peacefully on the banks of the Chandrabhaga river, and plays dwelling to a small temple of Vithoba. The temple was the brainchild of Umaji Aba, Diwan to Raja Baji Rao Bhonsle. This place is affectionately termed as the *Pandharpur of Vidarbha*. The nearest airport and rail head is at Nagpur, 36 kms from here. State Transport buses ply from Nagpur, Kalmeshwar, Saoner.

Bhadravati

Bhadravati also called Bhandak, is a historical village covering a great span of area, and is well known as a religious place for the Jains. There are various temples here that have been well maintained and possess paved marble flooring.

Main attraction here is the temple dedicated to Bhagawan Kesariyaji Parshvanath. Nearly 152 cms high, black-coloured idol of Bhagawan Kesariyaji Parshvanath in the semi-padmasana posture.

The four-mouth idol in the upper story of this splendid two-storeyed pinnacled temple, is very ancient and beautiful. In this single idol, there are reflections of the idols of Bhagawan Prabha Parshvanath, Prabhu Chandraprabh, and Prabhu Adinath. This is a special feature of this idol. There are many idols found here from the ground. Moreover, the remains found from the ruined buildings are artistically delightful

The ancient remains found from this tirth show that it is very ancient. Moreover, the archaeological department of the Govt. of India has declared this tirth as a protected memorial. In the year 1912 of the Vikram era, this tirth was entrusted by the Govt. to the Svetamber Jain Sangha. Impressed by seeing Kesariyababa, the then Governor of Madhya Pradesh, made on behalf of the Government a gift of 142 acres of land to the sangha for the use of the tirth. Then the sangha renovated the temple. In a dream a shravaka saw a Nagadevta in a temple and got an instruction to build a temple. Since the day on which the management of the temple was entrusted to the devotees according to the legend, the idol of Bhagawan came to be called Svapnadev Kesariya Parshvanath. Even today, many miracles happen here. On the tenth day of the dark half of the month of Magasar, a fair is held here every year.

A temple of Bhagawan Adinath and a Gurumandir besides this temple are there in the garden.

Nagpur has the nearest airport, at a distance of 123 kms, whereas the nearest railhead is Chandrapur 26 kms. State Transport buses ply from Nagpur, Chandrapur, Warora.

Pauni

Pauni is well placed on the Vainganga river and gets its name the mythical king Pawan. The land was a famous Buddhist centre from prehistoric times. The town envelopes an ancient fort with walls of stones, that are of a humungous size. The Murlidhara temple here holds great significance. Nagpur is 116 kms from here, the nearest railhead being Bhandara, which is at a distance of 61 kms from here. State Transport buses ply from Nagpur, Bhandara.

Muktagiri

Muktagiri is situated between two hills of Satpuda range near Achalpur of prehistoric significance, there exists a temple here housing the idols of Jain deities. Muktagiri has found a place in the holy Jain literature and thus is an important pilgrimage for the Jains. Among the idols of the Jain tirthankars are Parashnath, Mahavir etc. The king of Ellichpur (today's Achalpur) stared the construction of this temples in 11th century and the later rulers added to it. Today Muktagiri has more than one hundred temples in its complex. Some of them are also underground temples. The other attraction of this place is a 150 ft high Waterfall. But that did not deter the spirit of the devotees to construct temples. Thus one can see temples constructed across the bridge across waterfall. The statues of the Jain tirthankars are made up of either white or black marble. One can also find a rough replica of the rock-cut Kailash temple of Ellora at this place.

Ridhpur

Ridhpur is situated in the Morshi Taluka in Amravati district on the Chandur Bazaar-Morshi road. Ridhpur is the pilgrimage center for the Mahanubhav cult and is also known as 'Kashi of Mahanubhav cult followers' throughout the country. Thousands of pilgrims visit Ridhpur on Ashadh Pournima, Chaitra Pournima and Govind Prabhu Jayanti (August-September). Besides this, the holy place is visited by pilgrims in great numbers daily.

Shegaon

Shegaon, a municipal town in Khamgaon Tehsil is famous for the samadhi of Shri Gajanan Maharaj–a mystic saint as popular as Saibaba of Shirdi. You'll see a large number of Pilgrims here, some coming from distant parts of Western Maharashtra, Vidarbha. Allegorically, Shegaon can be described as the Pandharpur of Vidarbha. Thousands of devotees pay their respects at the Samadhi every Thursday, which is regarded as a special day.

See the temple of Shri Ram, also constructed in the premises of the shrine. If you visit Shegaon on Ram Navami in Chaitra and on the Hindu calendar, you can also attend the fair held here on these occasions.

Sindkhed Raja

Sindkhed Raja, a small Taluka place in Buldhana district, situated 105 kms, away from district headquarters on the state highway No. 183, is known world wide as the birth place of Rajmata Jijabai, the mother of the great Maratha warrior and king Chhatrapati Shivaji Maharaj.

There are a number of monument in this small township which owe their existence to Rajmata Jijabai and her father Lakhuji Jadhav, ancient temple of Neelkantheshwar and Rameshwar have great heritage and architectural value.

Badona-Ramnath

Main Deity–46 inches high idol of Bhagawan Adinatha.

The idol of Bhagawan Adinatha was installed in 1548. In addition to the idol of Bhagawan Adinatha we can find the idols of Choubis tirthankara and other Jain idols in this temple. People from different religion and different walks of life visit this temple to fulfill their wishes. This place is 22 Kms from Karanaja in Amaravati District.

Jintoor

Main Deity–6 feet 8 inches high idol of Bhagwan Neminatha.

This place was previously called as Jainpur. We can find a temple with Bhagawan Neminatha as the main deity. Six caves temples are situated on the hill. Apart from these we can find a temple with the attractive idols of Bhagwan Parshwanatha and Bahubali as the main deity. Since the idol of Bhagawan Parshwanatha in resting on a small stone this idol is also called as Antriksh Parshwanatha. The idols in this temple were installed under the guidance of Acharya Kumudchandra. An ancient temple of Rajulmati is also found at this place. It is said that thee were many Jain temples at this place but were invaded and destroyed by a Afghan person named Kadri who named this town as Jintoor. There are two temples in the village–Sahu Jain temple having 1000 idols and 2 mahavir Digambar Jain Mandir.

The hill is in the Sahyadari region 4 Kms from the village of Jintoor. Jintoor is at a distance of 45 Kms from Shirad-Shahapur.

The boarding and lodging facilities are available in the Dharamshala at sahu Jain Mandir.

Karanja

Main Deity–Idols of Bhagwan Parshwanatha and Bhagwan Chandraprabha.

Karanja is an ancient jain center. Earlier there were 3 Bhattarak Institutions (gaddi) known as 'Sengan-Kastha Sangh-Balatkatragan'. Three main temples of karanja are of these three maths. The first Jain temple belonging to Sengan is known as Sri Parshwanatha Digamabar Jain Sengan Mandir. The idol of Bhagwan Parshvanath is the main deity. Besides these 62 stone idols and 49 metal idols are found in this temple. The Samadhi of last Sengan Bhattarak Veersen is also here. A 500 years old painting showing the Panchakalayana is found in this temple. There is a manastambh in front of the temple and charans (footprints) of the Bhattarak are there. A rathyatra is taken out on the first day of the Krishna paksha of Chaitra month.

The temple of Kastha Sangh is dedicated to Bhagwan Chandraprabha in Padmasana. There are 6 stone and 10 metal idols on the vedi. Besides these, 29 metal and 31 stone idols are found in the kside vedi. The valuable Jain idols are kept in a room to the right of the Chandraprabha idol and to the left of Bhagawan Chandraprabha the idol of Godess Padmavathi is installed. This idol of Padmavathidevi is famous for its miracles. The yatra of Devi is taken out on the 15th day of bright moon of Chaitra month. The another special feature of this temple is a Mantap of 42 artistically decorated wood pillars.

The temple of Balatakar Sangh is dedicated to Bhagawan Chandranatha.This temple is called as 'Shri Mulsangh Chandranatha Swami Balatakagan Digambar Jain Mandir'. Besides the idol of Chandranatha, there are 11 metal and 2 stone idols on the vedi. 27 stone and 27 metals idols are found in the back vedi. The idol of Bhagwan Mahavir Swami in Padmasana is also very attractive. Two brass Sahasrakuta temples are found one of these has 1008 idols and the other has 1728 idols. Here the charan-padukae of bhattarak Devenderkirti are preserved.

The Mahavir Brahamacharayashram was established here by the inspiration of kshulakji Sri Parshwasagar. We can find a Mahavira temple and a museum at this ashram.

Karanja is 32 Kms from Murtijapur on Murtijapur-Yeotmal route. It is 62 Kms from Amravati. The lodging facilities are available in Sri Mahavir Brahmacharyashram.

NER

***Main Deity*–**Nearly 20 inches high, black coloured idol of Bhagawan Manovanchhit Parshwanatha in the Padmasana posture.

History says that the idol of Manovanchhit Parshwanatha of the city of Ner was brought here from Burhanpur. This idol is about 500 years old. It is said that the of Manovanchhit Parshvanath destroys unfulfilled desires of the devotees. This temple was renovated under the guidance of His Holiness Panyasapravar Surendravijayji on the tenth day of the bright half of the month of Vaishakha in the year 1988 of the Vikram era. This ancient tirth is also mentioned in the '908 Parshvanath Chhand'. A dharmashala, a bhojanshala and an upashraya are also found at this place.

The nearest railway station of Dhulia is at a distance of 27 kilometers from here and at a distance of 200 kilometers from Surat. Bus service and private vehicles are available to this place.

Shirpur

***Main Deity*–**Nearly 3 feet 7 inches high, black coloured idol of Bhagawan Parshwanatha in the Padmasana posture. We can find two Jain temples at Shirpur. One of these temples has the black coloured idol of Bhagawan Parshwanatha in the Padmasana posture. The idol in this temple is very ancient. This idol was installed by Mali and Sumali, the servants of Khaldusan, the brother-in-law of King Ravan. In the due course of time this temple was not seen for several years then it reappeared. It was reinstalled on the fifth day of the bright half of the month of Chaitra in the year 1715 of the Vikram era. On the fifth day of the bright half of the month of Magh in the year 1942 of the Vikram era it was installed in the new temple under the presence of Acharya

Abhaydevsurishvarji. In the due course of time this temple has under gone several renovations. It is said that this idol cures the diseases and solves the problems of the devotees, so devotees from different parts of the state visit this place. At the time of its installation the idol was at a horizontal distance of six fingers above the ground. A fair is held on the third day of the bright half of the month of Fagan and on then tenth day of the dark half of the month of Magasar. The other temple at this place is the beautiful artistic pinnacle temple of Bhagawan Vighnahara Parshwanatha.

Shirpur is at a distance of 19 kilometers from Wasim and at a distance of 72 kilometers from Akola. Bus service and private vehicles are available. Board and lodging facilities are available near the temple.

Salbardi

Salbardi is situated at just eight kms away from Morshi taluka in Amravati district. This place is associated with the mythological Ramayana era. It is said that Sita devi gave irth to her twins Luv and Kush here after being banished by Lord Rama and it is here, the win brothers captured the Aswamedha Yagna horse which was set free by Lord Rama. Salbardi is situated on the bank of Maru river. It is flanked by Satpuda ranage on all ides. There are two different streams flowing here – while one is cold the other is hot. People believe that a bath in these streams can cure skin ailments. The temple of Chakradhar swami also situated here. The Shiva temple of Salbardi is placed in a cave amidst Satpuda range. Since there is no motorable road one has to visit this temple on foot only. During the Mahashivratri devotees from far off places throng to this place to offer their prayers.The other attraction of Salbardi are the two huge man-made caves which are about 2000 years old.

Tapowaneshwar

Tapowaneshwar is situated at 15 kms away from Amravati at the confluence of three hills. Legends say that Rishi Rungi choosed this place to set up his ashram and later was invited by Lord Dasharath to perform *Putra Kamesti Yagna*. Since the place was used by Rishi Rungi for Meditation or *Tap,* thus the name of this place came to be known as Tapowaneshwar. There is a temple is this place in which the *Shiva Linga* is 3000 years old. Each Monday in the month of Shrawan (July-Sept) and Mahashivratri (Jan-April), more than 25,000 people gather for the festivals. Among the recent development of this place is a spiritual retreat set up by the Osho founadation.

Kondeshwar

Kondeshwar is 5 kms from Badnera. The main center of attraction here is the Shiva Temple. Legends say that King Vidarbha, after whom this region is named, on instruction of Rishi Kaundinya, constructed the Shiva Linga of this temple. The sculpted elephant on the walls of this temple is one of the best examples of Vidarbha's architecture. The surrounding hills and the serene river make this place a quiet and peaceful place. During the festivals on *each Monday in the month of Shrawan (July-Sept.) and Mahashivratri (Jan.-April), there is a rush of devotees.*

Nerpinglai

Nerpinglai is on the way to Salbardi, on a hillock. The Godess here is said to fulfill the wishes of her followers. But what makes Nerpinglai apart from other temples is that the Godess here has many Muslim followers too!!! During *Navratra Mahotsav from 1'st to 9'th of Ashwin Shukla (September-October).*

Bahiram

Bahiram is 23 kms from Achalpur. There still exist a doubt about the faith to which the deity of the shrine belong to. Both Hindu and Muslim pray at this shrine with equal piety. Being situated in hills, the scenic beauty of Bahiram attracts nature lovers too. There is a lake which is filled once in every three years. It is believed that River Ganga comes to this tank once in three year. One can also find pieces of temple architecture lying here and there at this place. Every *Kartik Paurnima Shirsha, Shukla 6 and the month of Pausha the festival at Bahiram attracts more than 50,000 devotees.*

Kaundanyapur–Deurwada

It is 35 kms from Amravati. Kaundanyapur and Deurwada are situated on either side of Purna river.

Kaundinyapur finds mention in the Great Indian Epic Mahabharat as the capital of Bhima, father of Rukmini. Lord Krishna eloped with Rukmini from this place. There is an ancient Shiva temple here. A big festival is organized from Kartik Shukla 15 (Full Moon Day) for one week. People from far off places take part in this festival and seek blessings of the Lord.

Deurwada is said to be the meeting place of Purna, Megha and Saraswati river. In ancient literature Purna river has been addressed as Payoshni river. Being in the confluence of three rivers there are 18 pilgrim centers in Deurwada itself and which are mentioned Hindu mythology. Very recently a huge stone-piece containing 12 *shiva lingas* together has been discovered. For this reason, it is denoted as *Chhoti Kasi*. All the 45 places mentioned in the Mahanubhav religious texts are present in Deurwada and thus it draws devotees from as far as Delhi, Haryana and Punjab. One such temple is Kajaleshwar Temple where even Govind Prabhu Chakradhar swami visited some 800 years back.

Someshwar Shiva Temple (Chandrapur)

Rajura taluka in Chandrapur district is well known as agricultural and commercial town. But the presence of Someshwar temple has also placed it as an important historical place. this temple was constructed by the king of yadav dynasty in 13th century A.D. He was a Brahmin and follower of hemadpanthi. The hemadpanthi followers worshipped lord Shiva everyday just after morning bath. Therefore the in order to offer his daily prayers built this temple, but what attracts tourist to this temple is more than just pilgrimage center, the images and sculptures are unique and beautiful which the state government declare it a protected monument in 1995.

Bazargaon (Nagpur)

Forty kms from Nagpur on the way to Amravati there is a village named Bazargaon.We can find temples dedicated to both Hindu and Jain deities. The Hindus temples are in hemadpanthi style and are the bhosle era. It also has a beautiful lake the Bhavani temple of Bazargaon is about 700 years old. These apart, there are a lot of small temples around Bazargaon. Thus it is named as the *"temple village."*

Sawanga (Amravati)

Sawanga village is situated in Pohra taluka of Amravati district there is a temple dedicated to lord Vittal. But what surprises the visitor is that unlike any other temple there is no elaborate puja rituals in the temple. The only way to venerate the lord is by burning camphor (kapur) legends says that the local Sant Avadhut Maharaj was the incarnation of lord Krishna and after his death his body vapourized like a camphor. From then on the only ritual practiced here in burning of camfor.

Sawanga is worth visiting on "GudhiPadwa" Marathi new year on this day camfor worth 4 to 5 lakh of rupees are burnt at a time. All the devotees supposed to buy camfor from the local market and not carry them from home. The second attraction of the day is the covering of a pole 73 ft. high which is regarded as symbol of Avadhut Maharaj. The only men now quite old, who does this work climbs the pole unrobing the old cloth and comes down robin it with new one. It is also believed that a visit to this temple is a boon for people suffering from "Jadutona". So on gudhi padwa day thousands suffering from such disorder gather here in the hope to find a cure. This very scene is the third attraction of that day.

Shri Keshetra Kapileswar (Gavhankund)

It is situated in Tembhurkheda village in Varud taluka of Amravati district. The main attraction of this is a swayambhu" or Natural Shiva Linga. The shiv linga is in the entrance of tunnel in satpuda range on the bank of Shakti River. A naturally carved nine-hooded snake is on the shiv linga and around it. it is said that this snake is the water–incarnation of Kapil muni and thus the name of the place. Devotees consider this linga as one of the jyotirlinga" there are seven tanks–while two are in front of the Kapilaswar temple and 5 are across river Shakti. Since the place is confluence of three rivers namely Savitri, Lakshmi, Shakti, this is regarded as a triveni sangam. In the Hindu month of shravana, devotees from all over Vidarbha and neighbouring state throng to this place. Maharashtra State Government play special buses to clear the festival rush.

Kalamb (Yawatmal)

It is an ancient village situated on *Nagpur Yavatmal* road. There is a typical underground temple dedicated to *Chintamani*. There is a famous water tank as *'Ganesh Kunda'*. The village is situated on the bank of river *Chakravati*. The fair of Shir Chintamani is held in the month of *Magh Shudha from Chaturthi to Saptani.*

Wani (Yawatmal)

Wani is tahsil headquarter situated on the bank of *Nirguda* river. The famous temple of *Shir Ranganath Swami* is in this town. Thousands of pilgrams visit the temple from Falguna vadi to Chitra Sud 15. Wani is an important center of trade in cattle and bullocks. There are *Coal Mines* near Wani. The place is well connected with important places in the district by state roadways and also by Rail.

Shri Nrusinha Saraswati Temple Karanja (Lad)

Shri Nrusinha Saraswati Temple Karanja (Lad) is situated 70 Km towards south from Amravati. Along with Amravati (Oomraooti) and Achalpur (Elichapur), Karanja (Lad) was one of the rich city and business centre during 17th century. Shri Nrusinha Saraswati is termed as the incarnation of Lord Dutta Guru in Indian Mythology. He worked for bringing light in the life of poor people. Karanja (Lad) is his birth place. Avery beautiful and attractive marble idol is placed in the Temple. People from all corner of Maharashtra visit this temple. The Darshana here is the experience of real mental peace. The festivities are in the month of January-February during Shri Nrusinha Saraswati Maharaj's Jayanti. Celebrations last for more than a week.

Rawanwadi (Buldhana)

Rawanwadi

This place is famous for a more than hundred year old Temple dedicated to Rama constructed by Shri Sitaram Prasad Dube a resident of Gunthara village on a hillock. On Ekadashi/ Amawasya day of kartik month, religious gathering takes place here. On the both sides of the tank there is dense forest which has converted it into not only a tourist and picnic spot but also a bird sanctuary.

Suryadeo Mando Devi

26 Kms from Gondia, in Goregaon Tehsil. Temple of Mando Devi (Reincarnation of Godess) situated over hillocks worshipped by devotees specially in navratra. Temple of Suryadeo (Sun God) situated on nearby hillock, picturesque location of tank.

Shri Rashtrasant Tukadoji Maharaj Temple, Gurukunj Mozari

Shri Rashtrasant Tukadoji Maharaj Temple, Gurukunj Mozari, is situated 39 km away from Amravati on Amravati-Nagpur section of national highway 6. This is a holy place graced by the residence of Rashtrasant Tukadoji Maharaj.The Ashrama was instituted by himself. He actively participated in the struggle for freedom movement and also motivated a large number of his follower to take part in it. He was in lime light during "Jungle Satyagraha." After freedom he enlightened the masses against the social evils. He wrote "Gramgeeta" which set the regulations for ideal development of rural persona and development of village itself. Other than his samadhi other temples are his Dhyana Mandir the meditation hall and all religion temple on nearby das tekadi. The festivities are in the month of October-November during his Jayanti.

Shri Maruti Temple, Changapur

Maruti Temple Changapur is situated in the outskirts of Amravati on Amravati-Paratwada road. This is Lord Hanuman Temple. Every Saturday large number of people visit this temple. The festivities are in the month of Feburary-March during Lord Hanuman Jayanti. The season is pleasant during this time and number of people host Vanbhojana here.

Shri Ganesh Temple, Vaygaon

Shri Ganesh Temple, Vaygaon is situated 15 Km from Amravati. This Temple is Lord Ganesh Temple build in 15th Century. According to records available and trusties, the foundation stone of this Temple was laid on the same day when Shri Shivaji Maharaja, First Mararta King was ceremoniously took his office.

HISTORICAL PLACES OF VIDARBHA

Balapur

Named after the goddess Baladevi, Balapur in Akola District has over the years turned into a seat of pilgrimage and a tourist spot. Located between the two rivers Mana and Mhais, it is placed at a distance of six km form the railway station.

The temple Baladevi, gave the place its name—Balapur. The fact that even Bal Krishnabua, the disciple of Samarth Ramdas Swamy, the 17th century saint was a native if this place adds to the importance of this town.

The place was known even before the Moughals had established their empire in India. According to the historians, Azim Shah, son of Moughal emperor Aurangzeb is known to have stayed there.

Also a commercial centre of some significance, the place was known in the earlier times for its people who manufactured paper and produced good quality "satranjis". It is a different story that these things have no takers today. That also explains why the people here live a neglected life.

The place is roughly divided in two Balapur peth and Balapur city. The fort and canopy of Raja Jai Singh in Balapur explains its historical significance The fort has been constructed over a hill near the confluence of the two rivers Mana and Mhais.

The fort is constructed with bricks which add to its glory and beauty. Except for the forts ion Melghat, nowhere else in Vidarbha one gets to see such magnificently constructed fort. The carvings on the fort are too good. The stone made canopy of Raja Jai Singh is a major tourist attraction. About 25 ft in height, the canopy gives an imposing look. Despite the historical importance, the natural scenic beauty, the magnificent fort and canopy and the religious importance of the place, the place is neglected reflecting on the apathy of the state government. What is needed is sincere efforts to develop the place and tap its tourism potential. Will that ever be taken care of is to be seen.

Naranala Fort

The Naranala Fort is also worth giving a shot. Located in the Akola district, it has been well maintained, possessing a fortress wall and beautiful bastions. Narnala is situated in Melghat at attitude 21°10' North and 77°00' East. It is 66 km. North from Akola. Narnala is 3161 feet from MSL. Fort was built scientifically considering natural interference like rain winded. Narnala alias shahanur fort consist of three small forts namely Zafrabad. Narnala and Teliagarh. Narnala is on one hour walling distance from Shahanur, 24 km from Akot (Akola). Now, there is a road from Akot via Popatkhed for vehicles.

This is historically very famous fort which is very deep and with dense forest land situated on the hills of Satpuda i.e. at the hilly side of the Melghat. (Narnala is at 24 km from Akot and 66 km from Akola on North). Noway's we can reach to fort by vehicle.

There is confusion about the consturction of Narnala fort. The historian finished have said that-Nineth Badshaha Shahbudeen Ahmadhaha Wali.(1422 AD to 1436 AD) constructed of Gawilgarh fort and made renewation in Narnala fort when he stayed at Elichpur. It means that the Narnala fort have constructed before Bahamany rule. Still it is not conform exactly when it is constructed as the concreate information not available anywhere.

Some historians have said that the Gond rules ruling over Melghat region constructed this fort (original owner). But this is also not supported by all the historian. After the Ahmadshaha second (1436 to 1458) become the ruler. He had got married with the daughter Nashirkhan (subedar of Khandesh). Due to misunderstanding between Allaudin and his wife. Nashirkhan made affable of Berar Region in 1453 A.D. he defeated first to the Gond. Gond living in Chorda and started his rule over Chorda fort. Then by motivating some sardar of Berar region he strengthen his provision of attack over Narnala fort. Nashirkhan achived many expectations. He had motivated the Elakhandipari of Berar and leader of army. By this provision Nashirkhan easily took change over Narnala fort in 1453 A.D.

Nagardhan

Nagardhan is an old town and was formerly of considerable importance as it gave its name to the district. It was founded by a Suryawanshi King, but noted hisorian Mr. Hiralal supposes it to have been established by King named Nandvardhan belonging to the Shail Dynasty. There is a fort said to have been built by the Bhonslas with brick walls.

Pavnar

Pavnar, of extreme historical importance, is strategically located in the district of Wardha on the verge of the Dham river. It forms one of the most prehistoric colonies in the district and gets its name from a renowned Rajput King by name Pravarasena. Pravarasena II founded a new city which the named Pravarapura, where he shifted his capital some time after his eleventh regional year. Some of his later land-grants were made at the new capital. He built there a magnificent temple of Ramachandra evidently at the instance of his mother who was a devout worshipper of Visnu. Some of the sculptures used to decorate this temple have recently been discovered at Pavnar on the bank of the Dham, 9.656 km. (6 miles) from Wardha, and have thus led to the identification of Pravrapura with Pavnar.

Of the few attractions that can be found here, are the Gandhi Kuti and the Paramdham Ashram of Vinobaji, the Sarvodaiya leader who launched the bhoodan movement. The latter is situated at a distance of 13 kms from the main land of Wardha.

Sevagram

Sevagram, again from the Wardha district, bore the name Shegaon earlier. It is believed that this place had the honour of being the headquarters of the social service programmes that Gandhiji conducted. It gets its name thus. Sewa means service and Gram means village. There also exists a Gandhi Ashram and a Gyan Mandir.

Shegaon is a small village near Wardha town (8 km). In spite of many practical difficulties, Gandhiji decided to settle here. He reached the village on the 30th April, 1936 early in the morning at about 5 a.m. He remained here for about five to six days. He called the villagers and the purpose of his visit and sought their permission to settle down here. He had no intention to keep anybody with him except his wife Kasturba. However slowly slowly pressure of work necessitated permission to more colleagues till Sevagram Ashram also became a full-fledged institution.

Gandhiji observed all the rules of Sabarmati Ashram here also. He was 67 years when he came to Sevagram. In those days the village was surrounded by forest on all sides. Snakes and scorpions were a common feature. There was only one footpath or cart track to Wardha. No post-office or telegraph office existed. There letters used to be brought from Wardha. There is another village in this region named Shegaon, made famous by the residence of Saint Gajanan Maharaj. Hence Gandhiji's letters used to get misdirected. Therefore, it was decided in 1940 to name this village as SEVAGRAM or the village of service.

Nagpur is 88 kms from here. Wardha, which also incidentally forms the nearest railhead to this place, is 9 kms. Mumbai is placed at a distance of 830 kms from Sevagram. Accommodation is also available at Yatri Niwas, MTDC also has a beautiful resort at Wardha.

Viragadh

The dilapited fort of Viragadh is situated at a distance of 14 kms from Armori village in Gadhchiroli district. King Kurumpramod of Naga dynasty built it, in 2nd century. the fort is spread across an area of 10 acres and the moat around the fort is 15 to 20 feet deep. It has three entrances and each entrance is beautifully sculpted with Lord Ganesh and other Hindu deities. It has six domes and each pillar has carvings depicting the life style of people in this era. There are four wells inside the fort and each of them there are statues of Lord Varun. This statues is an unique example of gond style of architecture. There are hidden ways inside the fort.

It is assumed that the fort must have been called Vajragadh (the hardest of the fort) but with passage of time the name was diluted to Vairagadh. Anther interesting fact also associated with the fort is that the princess of this region named "Ghushita" married the king of Utkal Kharvela King Kharvela ruled in Utkal around 2nd century B.C. and thus this fort must be as old as that.

Manikgadh Fort

This fort is situated at 12 km Gadhadur taluka in Chandrapur district. This was built by King Dahilu of Naga dynasty at 2200 ft. Above the sea level. Later Gond rulers had the possession of this fort. Currently this fort is in donce forest and it is dangerous to venture alone. Though different dynasties ruled this fort in different time, but no one ruled over it last 200/250 years. Thus it houses tigers, bears, snakes and the like animals, all the entrances of this fort are beautifully sculpted and it is assumed that the fort spread across five acres was built part by part by different dynasties and in different times. thus the architecture is a mixture of Naga, Gond, Mana, dynasty. The presiding deity of this fort is Danteshwar Devi of Bastar district in Chhattisgarh. This is the largest and the best fort in Chandrapur. The development of this fort will not only benefit Vidarbha and Maharashtra but the neighbouring, Andhra Pradesh and Chhattisgarh. Being situated in forest area this fort can be used to adventure.

Pratapgadh (BHANDARA)

Situated 2900 ft. above sea level is Pratapgadh in Bhandara district. Though little is known about who built this fort, the fort is worth paying a visit due to its natural surroundings. Inside the fort there are shrines of both Hindus and Muslims. This proves that this fort must have been occupied by both Hindu and Muslim rulers in different periods of history. The Garuda Stambh at the entrance has a unique architecture on stone. The deep and strait valleys around the fort act as a moat and were a natural hindrance for the enemies. The whole fort was built without the limestone. The height of this fort enables us to have a bird's eye view of the surrounding area. One can see Itoadoh dam, the canal, and tiled houses of the locals across the backdrop of greenery, which gives a breathtaking view.

Ambagadh (BHANDARA)

Situated in Bhandara district, Ambagadh is a fort, which has the unique Gond style of architecture. The center of attraction in this fort, is the entrance gate, the tower at the each corner and the underground jail. The entrance gate is so nicely carved that once falls in love with it at the very first sight. The towers are constructed in the minaret style and one of the best example of Gond sculpture. Gond and Bhosle rulers used the underground jail. It is compared with the "BhulBlaiya" of Gwalior fort. There were separate portions to keep elephant and horses. It also houses a small temple and a lake inside it. It is believed that this fort must have been built by Gond dynasty in 1690 AD. But today it is in dilapated condition and needs urgent attention for protection.

Shri Keshetra Chandpur (BHANDARA) 6.12.03

The prime attractions of Chandpur in Tumsar taluka of Bhandara district are the Mud dam built by the British and the ancient hanuman temple. The temple has a 7 feet high statue of Hanuman was the worshipper of Lord Rama. Four melas or fairs are held in a year in this temple and devotees gather in large numbers. It is believed that Swami Samarth Ramdas, the spiritual guru of Chatrapati Shivaji, also visited this temple. Just apposite the temple on the other side of lake there is a dargah dedicated to Bakhth Chand Shah Vali and thus Muslims too visit this place in equal numbers.

The reservoir formed by the Mud dam has been beautifully developed into a tourist resort. The there are a boating facilities but only paddleboats as they are eco friendly motor boats would have polluted the lake. Apart from that there are eco friendly restaurants, children's park; toy train etc. special cottages are built to stay near the lake. The old British age rest house has also been renovated. Being surrounded by thick greenery there are abundant flora and fauna. Trekking is also organized on regular basis.

Ambhore (BHANDARA)

Ambhore in Bhandara district is the meeting place of 5 rivers namely Kanhan, Ainganga, Pench, Amn, and Sur. On this meeting place is famous Chaitaneshwar temple needles to say that this place is full of scenic beauty. This place also has the memorial of first Marathi Poet Mukundraj Raghunath.

Dhas Waterfall (BHANDARA)

It is in Dewari taluka near Chichgadh gaon on the Gadhvi River. The center of attraction in dhas is the huge waterfall and the scenic beauty around it. The jungle dogs of this region are ferocious and they always stay in a group. A group, of such dogs hunts tiger. There is a mention of these dogs in the Vedic literature where they were called as "MANCHAL". However, today these dogs are an endangered specis. Surabhi TV serial mention this place in one of its episode.

Chimur (CHANDRAPUR) 21.9.03

Chimur in Chandrapur district has caves where one can find stone paintings of early man. Historian. Ganesh Halkare discovered these paintings in Satbahini hills of Chimur and studied them. According to him these paintings are more than 5000 years old, which is the oldest Cave paintings in Vidarbha. The other attraction of Chimur is a cave, which has statue of Sitadevi. Another place called Shankarpur near Chimur has drawn the attention of researchers as the Graveyards of ancient men were excavated here. The graveyard is divided into two parts. While one part contained the body, the other part contained the items the dead men like.

Papamiyan Tekdi (CHANDRAPUR) (for Study)

Situated 3 km away from Chandrapur on the way to Mul, one finds Papamiyan Tekdi (hill) the stone weapons found on this hillocks is said to be 15000 years old and belongs to stone age. The whole hillock is like anthropological museum, which takes us back to stone age.

Kachargadh (BHANDARA) 28.7.03

On the Bhandara raipur highway between Salekasa and Darekasa railway station lies Kacharagadh natural cave. The cave is big enough to accommodate 400 to 500 people comfortably. This cave was inhabited by the ancient human being some 50000 years ago. The stone weapons found in the caves prove this. The cave is surrounded by natural beauty and the Hazrafall is only eight kms from this cave.

Padampur

30 Kms from Gondia in Amgaon Tehsil. Bhavbhuti, the great Sanskrit litterateur was born here. He wrote famous Sanskrit drama Malti Madhav, Mahavir Charita and Uttar Ram Charita. Historical and ancient idols are found here.

Dakram Sukdi

40 Kms from Gondia in Tiora Tehsil. It is famous for Chakradhar Swami Temple visited by Mahanubhav Panth followers. Chaitra Mela in the month fo April.

Kamtha

15 Kms from Gondia, place of historical importance being administrative headquarters of Kamtha Zamindari (covering most of the Gondia district) in last century. Famous for Shiv temple build by lacal saint Lahri Baba, visited every Thursday by devotees specially on Guru Purnima.

The Living Culture

The culture of people finds its vivid expression in their festivals and folklore, performing arts, costumes, cuisines and their style of living.

Festivals

Hindu life is replete with celebration of all kinds. There are holidays and other religious festivals and birthday anniversaries of various deities and mythological heroes, which as a rule are observed every year.

Gudi Padva, Rama Navami, Hanuman Jayanti, Ashadhi and Kartiki Ekadashis, Gokulashtami, Poda, Ganesh Chaturthi, Gauripujan, Dussehra, Diwali, and Holi, are the main holidays which are celebrated with enthusiasm.

"Dussehra and Diwali" are the most important festivals of this area. They are national festival also. So they are celebrated all over India with equal enthusiasm. But "Ganesh festival", "Pola" are typically festivals of Vidarbh. Ganesh festival is celebrated privately and publicly all over Vidarbha. Gudhi padva, Gokulashtami, Naralipoornima, holi poornima are also the days of festivity for Vidarbha. The religious minded people of Vidarbha observe Shivaratri, Ashadhi Ekadashi and Kartiki Ekadashi as fasting days.

Among Muslims Muharram, Ramzan Id and Bakr-Id festivals and some other fairs are observed. As in other parts of India, Moharram is celebrated with great in Vidarbha also. The Muslims celebrate this festival in commemoration of the great spiritual leaders of Islam-Hasan and Hussein who died as martyrs, and the noteworthy thing is that Hindus also take part in it.

Folklore

The folklore of the people is usually a part of their festivals. They celebrate these gay occasions by singing chorus songs and performing dances which tradition has handed down to them. Of the folk songs, Ovis and Gavlans are the most common and universal, sung usually by women when in gay, festive mood. Ovis describes in a simple and lucid manner the joys and sorrows of domestic life. The birth of the baby in the home, mothers deep endearment for her children, sisters attachment to her brother, the yearnings of a newly married girl for her mothers home, her bashful love for her husband and her trouble and adjustments with the life in her new home-these are the themes of Ovi songs. Their composers have remained anonymous, but their songs are handed down by one generation to another. Their simple beauty and exquisite charm have no parallel in Marathi folk literature. Gavlans are songs of Radha who registers her complaints about the mischief and naughtiness of Krishna and also her great love for the Lord of Gokul.

In some part of Vidarbh, villagers are interested in arranging "Natak, Tamasha" on the occasion of "Shankar-Pat" in the month of January and February and also arranges the culture programmes as "Dandar" on Festival days like Dushehra, Diwali, Holi etc. But nothing is like the tamasha of course. It reigns supreme among the folk arts of Vidarbha. Its overwhelming attraction for the Marathi mind can only be compared to the stage. In fact, the tamasha is a combination of song, drama and dance, set against the rural background. It usually consists of two parts, Gan-Gavlan and Vag. The former include the singing and dance, while latter is a story play, usually humorous and farcical. About six to eight persons, men and women form a tamasha troupe. The main female dancer is the central figure of the performance, while the songadya, or the clown, who is a humorous and ready witted player, provides all the fun.

If the Lavnis are songs of love, the Powadas are songs of the bravery of the Maratha warriors and soldiers, which are sung to the accompaniment of a Daf (a small size drum) and a Tuntuna (single string instrument). In fact the object of the Powada songs in the old days was to rouse people and stir them to action. Even today they never fail to thrill the masses by bringing back to their mind the glorious deeds and act of bravery and martyrdom of the heroes of the past.

Bharud, Lalits and gondhals are some other forms of folk art of Vidarbha. Bharud is a narration in verse of some home truths, more about mans spiritual life, garbed in wit and allegories. Lalits are a crude type of drama depicting mythological stories, while gondhalas are a song recitation by Gondhalis who area special of village bard, in praise of certain deities and narrating mythological stories.

Costume

There is little that could be written about the dress of the people. Men as a rule use white clothes, sometimes with a red turban that is folded. Cultivators use rough loin-cloth of strong and sturdy make. On the head they have a small piece of cloth, which they call *rumal*. Under the hear cloth. Men often wear little cotton caps.

Women wear one long cloth secured round the waist and folded over shoulders that is called sari when it has a silk border and a *lugde (Nauari)* when it has cotton borders. Nauari, the traditional saree with carved border got its name from being nine-yards in length. Ponwar, Dhimar, and Kohli women often wear white clothes, locally called *karvan*. Immigrants from the north as the Umre kalars, Bhaore Manas, Kirars and others wear the angia or breast-cloth tied behind while those of the south have the *choli* which is tied in front. However in present days the people in the cities have become fashion-conscious and modern to ultra morden dress.

Ornaments

Men hardly use any ornaments but among women they are popular. Even in this respect fashions have much changed and there is a desire to imitate people from cities like Nagpur. For Children, a number of bracelets, anklets and necklaces are used. They are of gold among well to-do but of silver among the poor.

The most distinct ornament in the Vidarbha culture is the *Nath*, the nose pin. Birya, the pearl ear tops; Ekdani, Chaplahar, Gahupot are the necklace varities; Patlya, the gold bangles with pearls are traditional ornaments worn by women. Mangalsutra, made of black beads and gold with pendant, is a symbol of wellbeing is wore by the married women.

Cuisine

Among the moth watering cuisines of Vidarbha are *Varan, Bhat, Chapati, Kadhi, Patovadya, Amtee, Ras-shivlya, Mande, Rodge replete* with *Koshimbir, Pickles and Papad*. The much famous non-vegeterain dish Varhadi Mutton is for those who like it hot and spicy.

During the festivities people make snacks like *Anarse, Chakli, Puranpoli, Shankar Pale, Modak, Kandpapdi, Karanji, Lado, Chivda* in large quantities and feed their guests.

The main couse is follwed by desserts like *Shrikhand, Basundi and Shira*. The hospitality of people of Vidarbha does not end here. After the food the guests are offered *Tambul*, a betel leaf preparation as digestive.

Cultivators in Vidarbh eat *ambil*, a gruel of boiled *jovari* and water at about ten and two O'clock. Tamarind vinegar is mixed with this to add to its relish and it is eaten with salt, onions and chillies. For the evening meal they have *bhakar* or thick *chapattis* made of Jvari with vegetable and pulse, or *besan*, i.e., gram flour cooked in water with salt, chillies and onions.

Most men smoke and a good many chew tobacco and some take it in the form of snuff. Women do not usually smoke but many of them chew tobacco.

The account of festivities in Vidarbha will not be complete without a mention of hurda parties. Hurda is jowar grain baked fresh when it is still in milk. As the jowar crop gets ready for harvest, farmers invite their friends and relatives for Hurda parties, which are held in the farm itself. fresh green jowar ear heads are plucked, baked in the fire and grain separated from the ears by rubbing them with hands. These are then served to the guests along with spices and curds. Hurda parties are in fact social gatherings of the village people held in celebration of the harvest.

Games and Sports

Of the various games and sports played in rural areas, wrestling is by far the most popular in Vidarbha fairly big village generally has a talimkhana, or gymnasium, where young man developed their physical strength by muscular exercises like Dandas and baithakas and other gymnastics. They keep their bodies trim by performing Mallakhamb acrobatics' wrestling bout is a very exciting part of the village fair, where young pehelwans from the surrounding villages come to grip in a trial of strength. The winners are awarded turbans and silver bracelets as prizes. They bring a fair name not only to themselves but to their village also

While Hututu (kabaddi as it is called in the north, Atyapatya, kho-kho and Lesim are games generally played by men, women have their special games like zimma and fugadis. Zimma is a simple dance in which about a half a dozen girls move swiftly and rhythmically in a circle keeping time by clapping of their hands and strokes of their feet, while singing a chorus song. In a fugadi, girls in batches of two, with their hands interwoven, revolve round and round of their heels at breath taking speed.

Tribal Culture

The tribals of Vidarbha have come in contact with the modern civilization but their culture still maintains a unique identity. In some areas they still wear nothing, stay in caves and depend on hunting and food gathering for their livelihood. They have good knowledge of medicinal plants and find cure for their ailments themselves.

The tribals in the district have their own culture. They are used to perform worships of their God “Persa Pen” and others.

They do dance "Rela" on auspicious occasions and when new crops come. Rela dance is popular dance among the tribals. The other dance is "Dhol" dance. Holi, Dushehra and Deewali are the main festivals of Korku tribes. The tribal community families reside in the dense forest of Vidarbh.

INFRASTRUCTURE–ACCESSIBILITY AND AMENITIES

The potential for development of tourism at a given destination depends as much on the availability of a *strong tourism resource* base, as on the *tourist plant facilities* in terms of accessibility, internal transportation, accommodation, recreation and entertainment provisions, travel agency and tour operations services, shopping opportunities and so on. However, *the state of basic infrastructure,* related to water and power supply, communication and currency exchange facilities, health-hygiene and security-safety services etc. seemingly more relevant from resident viewpoint, essentially acts as a decisive factor in the ultimate growth and development of tourism industry. Obviously, tourist may not feel impelled to visit a destination, which lacks in the basic infrastructure.

Putting it other way round, even the areas with lesser tourism resource potential but equipped with requisite support infrastructure has greater development potential than those with rich tourist resource treasure but very poor infrastructure. Promoting tourism in infrastructurally strong areas is more convenient both from time and money viewpoints. Naturally, potential tourism enterprises too, prefer to invest in such areas, in view of the lesser cost of development *vis-à-vis* possibility of access to a greater market segment. Fact remains that the quality of tourist plant facilities at a destination are necessarily determined by the quality of available basic infrastructure. Otherwise also, quality infrastructure has decisive impact on the economy as a whole as it acts as a strong stimulant to economic development besides effectively activating the latent entrepreneurship. Not only this, from resident view point, modernization of infrastructure leads to improvement in the living standard, enhancement in awareness and effective interaction with the out side world etc. in addition to expansion of trade and industries.

As such provision of requisite infrastructure at a given place/ area consumes considerable time to create and, involves substantial capital investment. Thus, it is generally expected that central and local government work on the infrastructure, since the supra-structure can subsequently be developed by the private sector.

Coming back to tourism, the infrastructural requirements are too diverse and at times too specific, depending on the type of touristic appeal and the range of tourist activities possible/or to be developed at a given destination. For example, trekking does not involve much of the infrastructure or tourist plant facilities, except a definitive trek and a guide, as also availability of suitable camping site(s) enroute. Likewise, river running, aero-sports and ice-skiing activities have their own set of requirement in term of basic infrastructure *vis-à-vis* tourist plant facilities. Interestingly, same tourist visiting different destination or travelling under different motive may have different set of demands guided by his/her purpose of visit *vis-à-vis* expectations with regard to the given destination.

Transportation

Consistent improvement in the accessibility facilities over the ages has had tremendous contribution in the all-round advancement of the civilization. Knowledge about the distant lands and people not only created more curiosity to see more but also broadened the horizons of awareness alongside creating opportunities for knowledge sharing or say progress sharing. As of now, the dramatic innovations in the means of travel, particularly in the air transportation, have resulted into steady narrow-down of the time-distance gap, thereby transforming the world into a closer neighbourhood. The contemporary concept of globalization, just not in the terms of trade and commerce, but also from socio-cultural viewpoints, can be largely attributed to the revolutionary developments on transportation front. The global tourism industry that thrives on mobility of people naturally owes its dramatic pace of growth to the effective and yet safer and cheaper means of travel available to the society. Democratization of transport facilities has further opened-up the travel opportunities for almost every section of the society–be it rich from an affluent country or a middle class from the developing world. Thus, suddenly the size of tourist market has multiplied thereby making tourism to be the fastest growing industry on planet earth. Evidently, the countries, regions and even individual destinations equipped with better accessibility facilities have better market share in tourism.

Today, new scientific inventions and innovations are fast changing the old orders as it inevitably yields place to new. Means of communication are fast developing and the state bus service has now reached even to the innermost part of the countryside.

Accessibility and basic amenities are two key ingredients for tourism development of any region. In Vidarbha too many of the tourist places are are not accessible. And wherever there ares amenities they are not optimally used. Chapter 6 of this study makes an elaborate assessment of the infrastructure and amenities of this region. Nonetheless, here is a brief preview of the amenitities.

The greatest advantage of Vidarbha is its central location, equidistant from all the four metros. Vidarbha is blessed with one of the best airports at Nagpur and soon it is going to become an international airport. It has got daily flight connection to Mumbai, Chennai, Delhi and Kolkata.

Nagpur again is major railway junction where all major south-north bound and east-west bound trains halt. It is an ideal break journey stop for those who are travelling from one end of the country to the other. Besides Nagpur the other major railheads of Vidarbha Akola, Wardha, Gondia, Tumsar also can be developed into entry points to the beautiful countryside.

Similarly, the road network is also well developed in Vidarbha. In fact, Maharashtra is one of the top states in India in terms of mettalled roads. However the current pattern is to connect major business centers. All one needs is to change the focus to connect the major tourist centers.

So far so, a detailed study on the amenities of this region is still awaited. One can only draw conclusions from the already available statistics on Maharashtra. Nine National Highways pass through Maharashtra with a total length of 2769 Kms. The total length of the State Highways is 30,548 Kms. Total length of railway line is 5614 Kms.

However the amenities in tourist places of Vidarbha speaks the sorry state of affairs. The Maharshtra Tourism Development Corporation (MTDC) has done a little to develop the amenities in tourist places of this region whereas it has a number of resorts in the western part of Maharashtra. The only MTDC resorts at Chikhaldara and Lonar are in dilapated condition for the want of maintenance. The private entrepreneurs need to come up with more accommodation units and enroute amenities. There are hardly any good restaurants in the places of tourist interest. Same is the state of telecom, banking and other related services.

Existing Tourist Profile, Traffic Trends and Resource Use Pattern

There is hardly any study available on the existing traffic trends of Vidarbha region. While MTDC collects the statistical data about the tourist traffic it has not commissioned any separate study on this region. Thus from the press reports and other unreliable sources it is estimated that 1,23,456 visitors came to Vidarbha solely for the purpose of Tourism. Out of this 345 were visitors of foreign origin. The foreign nationals came mainly to Lonar for a study before the NASA's Mars Exploration programme.

As stated earlier MTDC has only five properties in Vidarbha region, the details of which is given as under:

Destination	*Type of Accommodation*	*No. of Rooms*	*No. of Beds*	*Total Capacity*
Chikhaldara	Luxury Cottages	10	04	40
	Dormitories	01	30	30
Lonar	Standard Room	08	02	16
	Dormitory	02	16	32
Washim	Standarad Room	03	02	06
Tadoba	Standard Room	15	02	30
Ridhapur	Standard Room	04	02	08
Total		**43**	**58**	**162**

Looking at the poor show of the MTDC outlets the private entrepreneurs are shy of investing. Thus except at Chikhaldara there is not much private accommodation units in Vidarbha. Most of the tourist places are placed in natural areas and the strict forest laws come on the way of tourism promotion. Safety and security at these secluded places is another concern that bothers the private entrepreneurs. There is lack of local awareness about the boon that tourism can bring to that area.

USP of The Region

1. *Lonar:* The only meteoric impact crator in basaltic rock.
2. *Mansar:* The excavated Stupa here is bigger than the Sanchi near Bhopal.
3. *Chimur:* Cave paintings of the Paleolithic Man dating back to 600 B.C.
4. *Chandrapur:* Fossil remains of plants and animals of Cretacious period.
5. *Geetai Mandir, Wardha:* A unique attempt to put the teaching of Bhagvat Geeta on the stones in a natural surrounding.
6. *Remains of Shukracharya's School*: Learning Warfare near Lonar.
7. *Kachargarh Caves, Bhandara:* Has a capacity of accommodating 400-500 people. Was the place of community residence of early man.
8. *Mendha, Bhandara*: The only place in India where image of Lord Ganesh bears moustache, beard and worshipped as a hermit.
9. *Ambhore, Bhandara:* Meeting place of five rivers and houses Chaitaneswar temple.
10. *Hemalkasha, Chandrapur:* The first charity hospital for the wild animal in India where even the wildest animals behave in most friendly manner.
11. *Anandvan, Chandrapur:* Under the leadership of Baba Amte this village is set up and run by leprosy patients.
12. *Bairam, Amravati:* The lake here is filled with water only in alternative years.

4
Ongoing Efforts in Tourism

INTERPRETATION OF FINDINDS

Tourism development in Vidarbha is in its nascent stage. Thus most of the places described in the previous chapters have little or no accessibility. Due to constraints of time and money it was not practically possible to make a first hand survey. Same was the case with the secondary sources. Very little has been studied and written about Vidarbha separately. Thus the scholar had to draw conclusions from the data available for whole of Maharashtra. With the limited data that was available on Vidarbha from various publications and institutions, the scholar has tabulated the information and interpreted them using statistical analytical tools like graphs and pie chart.

Existing Tourism Infrastructure

The potential for development of tourism at a given destination depends as much on the availability of a *strong tourism resource* base, as on the *tourist plant facilities* in terms of accessibility, internal transportation, accommodation, recreation and entertainment provisions, travel agency and tour operations services, shopping opportunities and so on. However, *the state of basic infrastructure,* related to water and power supply, communication and currency exchange facilities, health-hygiene and security-safety services etc. seemingly more relevant from resident viewpoint, essentially acts as a decisive factor in the ultimate growth and development of tourism industry. Obviously, tourist may not feel impelled to visit a destination, which lacks in the basic infrastructure.

Putting it other way round, even the areas with lesser tourism resource potential but equipped with requisite support infrastructure has greater development potential then those with rich tourist resource treasure but very poor infrastructure. Promoting tourism in infrastructurally strong areas is more convenient both from time and money view points. Naturally, potential tourism enterprises too, prefer to invest in such areas, in view of the lesser cost of development *vis-à-vis* possibility of access to a greater market segment. Fact remains that the quality of tourist plant facilities at a destination are necessarily determined by the quality of available basic infrastructure. Otherwise also, quality infrastructure has decisive impact on the economy as a whole as it acts as a strong stimulant to economic development besides effectively activating the latent entrepreneurship. Not only this, from resident view point, modernization of infrastructure leads to improvement in the living standard, enhancement in awareness and effective interaction with the out side world etc. in addition to expansion of trade and industries.

As such provision of requisite infrastructure at a given place/ area consumes considerable time to create and, involves substantial capital investment. Thus, it is generally expected that Central and Local Government work on the infrastructure, since the supra-structure can subsequently be developed by the private sector.

Coming back to tourism, the infrastructural requirements are too diverse and at times too specific, depending in the type touristic appeal and the range of tourist activities possible/or to be developed at a given destination. For example, trekking does not involve much of the infrastructure or tourist plant facilities, except a definitive trek and a guide, as also availability of suitable camping site(s) enroute. Likewise, river running, aero-sports and ice-skiing activities have their own set of requirement in term of basic infrastructure *vis-à-vis* tourist plant facilities. Interestingly, same tourist visiting different destination or travelling under different motive may have different set of demands guided by his/her purpose of visit *vis-à-vis* expectations with regard to the given destination.

The region is full of touristic potential in the form of tribal life, historical forts etc. Alongwith the infrastructure needed for developing tourism in the Vidarbha region it is essential to understand and promote the existing potential of tourism in the region. The following table gives a brief overview of the rich and diverse tribal life in the region.

Transportation

Consistent improvement in the accessibility facilities over the ages has had tremendous contribution in the all-round advancement of the civilization. Knowledge about the distant lands and people not only created more curiosity to see more but also broadened the horizons of awareness alongside creating opportunities for knowledge sharing or say progress sharing. As of now, the dramatic innovations in the means of travel, particularly in the air transportation, have resulted into steady narrow-down of the time-distance gap, thereby transforming the world into a closer neighbourhood. The contemporary concept of globalization, not just in the terms of trade and commerce, but also from socio-cultural viewpoints, can be largely attributed to the revolutionary developments on transportation front. The global tourism industry that thrives on mobility of peoples naturally owes its dramatic pace of growth to the effective and yet safer and cheaper means of travel available to the society. Democratization of transport facilities has further opened-up the travel opportunities for almost every section of the society – be it rich from an affluent country or a middle class from the developing world. Thus, suddenly the size of tourist market has multiplied thereby making tourism to be the fastest growing industry on planet earth. Evidently, the countries, regions and even individual destinations equipped with better accessibility facilities have better market share in tourism.

Airways

Nagpur is the sole domestic airport of Vidarbha. Besides state owned Indian Airlines and its subsidiary Alliance Air private carriers like Jet Airways also operate their flight to and from Nagpur. Currently, it s connected daily to the State Capital Mumbai and National Capital Delhi. It also connects weekly thrice to Bhubaneswar, Kolkata and Hyderabad.

Tribal Life at a Glance

Sl. No.	*Name of the Tribe*	*Profession*	*Jewelleries*	*Dance*	*Music Instrument*	*Ghotul System*	*Types of Marriage*
1	*2*	*3*	*4*	*5*	*6*	*7*	*8*
1.	Gond	Hunting & Farming	Made of different metal, glass & *lakh.* *Bagdya, Mala, Wade, Karnafule, Sariya.*	*Dhemsa Dhemsa Ghorpad*	*Bansri, Duf, Ghungroo*	Yes	Marriage by Capture/ intrusion
2.	Koruku	Shifting Cultivation	Made of Silver, Shells, *Kaudi.* Glass beads. *Satra, Pairi, Bicha, Mundi, Kada, Bigdi.*	Gof,	*Pagai, Duf, Mardal*	No	Marriage by Purchase/ Service
3.	Madia	Hunting & Farming	Made of Glass and *Pital.* *Julki, Naini, Waki, Gajli, Painjan, Bari, Mudra.*	*Dhol, Rela*	*Duf, Dhol, Mridang*	Yes	Marriage by Trial/intrusion
4.	Halba	Pastoralist	Made of Silver, Shells, *Kaudi.* Glass beads. *Satra, Pairi, Bicha, Mundi, Kada, Bigdi.*	*Ghangadi*	*Ghangadi, Tarpa*	Yes	Marriage by Mutual Consent

Contd...

1	2	3	4	5	6	7	8
5.	Bhil	Animal Breeders	Made of Silver, Shells, Brass and Stone *Baliya, Hasli, Mala, Nathi, Haar.*	*Dhol, Ghangadi*	*Kathya, Dera*	No	Marriage by trial
6.	Banjara	Herdsmen	Made of Ivory, Animal Horns and bones. *Wale, Paingan, Bangdiya*	NIL	*Tuntune, Kingri*	No	Marriage by elopement
7.	Kolam	Artisan	Made of Silver. *Jodvi, Mangalsutra, Patlya, Bajubandh, Kudya, Tordya, Karnafule.*	*Dof, Ghorpad*	*Chitkora, Tiprya,*	Yes	Marriage by service
8.	Korwa	Cultivator	(Made of Silver) *Mungamala, Bers, Nakhuti Paira, Bichiya Terkula*	*Rela*	*Jhanz, Kuddi*	No	Marriage by exchange
9.	Thakar	Food gatherers	Made of Ivory, Animal Horns and bones. *Wale, Paingan, Bangdiya*	NIL	*Bana, Dhol*	Yes	Marriage by mutual consent
10.	Pardhan	Farming	Made of different metal, glass and *lakh*. *Bagdya, Mala, Wade, Karnafule, Sariya.*	NIL	*Tasha, Ghungroo, Lezim*	No	Marriage by service

Forts at a Glance

Sl. No.	Name of the Fort	District	Period	Famous for	Conservation By ASI	Guiding Facility	Transport	Accommodation
1.	Balapur	Akola	17th Century AD	Stone Carvings	No	No	By Bus	At Akola
2.	Narnala	Akola	1422 AD	War Fort	No	No	By local transport	At Akola
3.	Vairagarh	Amravati	2nd Century AD	Gond Architecture	No	No	By local transport	At Chikhaldara
4.	Manikgarh	Chandrapur	17th Century AD	Adventure activities	No	No	No	At Chandrapur
5.	Pratapgarh	Bhandara	NA	Natural Surrounding	No	No	No	At Bhandara
6.	Ambagarh	Bhandara	1690 AD	Bhul-Bhulaiya & entrance gate	No	No	By Bus	At Bhandara
7.	Sitabuldi Fort	Nagpur	1857 AD	Central Location	No	Yes	By local transport	At Nagpur
8.	Gavilgarh	Amravati	12th Century AD	Tunnel to Narnala fort	No	Yes	By Bus	At Chikhaldara

Touristic Appeal—District-Wise

Districts	*Historical Importance*	*Wildlife*	*Tribal*	*Religion*	*Nature*	*Wetland*	*Shopping*	*Handicraft*
Akola	+	+	+	+	+	+	-	-
Amravati	+	+	+	+	+	+	+	+
Bhandara	-	+	+	+	+	+	-	-
Buldhana	+	+	+	+	+	+	-	-
Chandrapur	+	+	+	+	+	-	-	-
Gadchiroli	-	+	+	+	+	-	-	+
Gondia	-	+	+	+	+	+	-	-
Nagpur	+	+	+	+	+	+	+	+
Wardha	+	+	-	+	+	-	+	+
Wasim	+	-	-	+	-	-	-	-
Yavatmal	-	+	+	+	+	-	-	+

\+ Presence of the Tourism Product
\- Absence of the Tourism Product

Departure Schedule

From Nagpur to	*Days of Operation*	*Flight No.*	*Departure*	*Arrival*
Bhubaneswar	Mo / We / Fr	CD-7276	1935	2050
Delhi	We / Su	IC-872	0800	0915
	Mo / Fr	IC-872	0800	0925
	Tu / Th / Sa	IC-869	0920	1045
Hyderabad	Mo / We / Fr	CD-7275	1635	1735
Kolkata	Mo / We / Fr	CD-7276	1935	2215
Mumbai	Daily	CD-7130	0825	0940
		9W-112	0855	1010
		9W-116	2130	2250
		IC-630	2135	2250

Arrival Schedule

To Nagpur From	*Days of Operation*	*Flight No.*	*Departure*	*Arrival*
Bhubaneswar	Mo / We / Fr	CD-7275	1440	1605
Delhi	We / Su Mo / Fr Tu / Th / Sa	IC781 IC569	0550 0550	0715 0845
Hyderabad	Mo / We / Fr	CD-7276	1805	1905
Kolkata	Mo / We / Fr	CD-7275	1315	1605
Mumbai	Daily	CD-7129 9W-111 9W-115 IC-829	0640 0705 1940 1940	0755 0825 2055 2055

Road

Vidarbha can boast of one of the finest road links in the country. Located right at the heart of India it has got road connection to the four corners of the country. The Dhule–Kolkata National Highway No. 6 connects Vidarbha to Mumbai in the west and Kolkata in the east. Similarly, the ambitious North-South corridor project connects Vidarbha to Jammu in the north and Kanyakumari in the south. The same corridor also connects Vidarbha to cities like Chandigarh, Delhi, Agra, Gwalior, Jhansi, Bhopal in the north and Hyderabad, Bangalore, Salem in the south. Within Vidarbha region also the road network is quite developed. All the district headquarters are well connected to each other. While the entire tourist destinations discussed in the previous chapter may not have good road connections, the major ones like Chikhaldara-Melghat and Lonar certainly do.

Railways

Two main broad gauge lines Delhi–Chennai and Mumbai–Kolkata intersect at Nagpur making it the super railway hub of the country. Being equidistant from and well connected by super fast trains to all the four metropolitan is the biggest advantage of Nagpur.

New Delhi–1091 RKM	Howrah–1139 RKM
Chennai–1099 RKM	Mumbai–830 RKM

In fact, it can be broadly observed that air transport facility in the region is still in its primitive stage but further developments in this regard need to be carefully planned taking into account the likely socio-economic and environmental cost-benefit of the same.

Accommodation

Like transport, accommodation too is vitally important component responsible for growth and development of tourism. Availability of appropriate accommodation facilities for various categories of travelers has determining impact on the type and volume of tourist traffic to a given destination/destination region. The type of touristic appeal and tourist use patterns *vis-à-vis* motivation and socio-economic and cultural perspectives of the effective and potential tourists, on the other hand, closely guide the type of accommodation facilities. Provision of requisite accommodation is also vitally important enroute as much at the destination.

As observed in the foregoing, tourist motivation and touristic use-patterns have vital bearing on the provision of accommodation.

No. of Beds in Accommodation Units at Major Tourist Destination

Place	*District*	*MTDC**	*PWD**	*FDCM**	*Hotels**	*Others**
Chikhaldara	Amravati	34	04	10	18	20
Lonar	Buldhana	18	06	08	10	25
Washim	Washim	02	04	Nil	12	12
Tadoba	Chandrapur	02	06	15	18	12
Ridhapur	Amravati	02	Nil	Nil	10	28
Shegaon	Akola	06	10	Nil	15	30
Navegaon Bandh (Nagzira)	Bhandara	06	04	06	10	15

Source: Vidarbha Sanshodhan Sansthan, Nagpur.

**MTDC Travellers' Lodge/Tourist Lodge/*
**PWD Guest Houses*
**FDCM Rest House*
**Hotels*
**Others Rain Baseras, Dharmshalas, Ashrams and Gurudwaras, Paying Guest Accommodation.*

Other Roadside Amenities

Apart from transport and accommodation, fast food outlets, eating houses, restaurants, motels, tourist information centers, health centers, toilets, drinking water, communication network, safety and security provisions, auto repair workshops and petrol pumps etc. are integral part of the roadside tourist amenities especially significant in the context of tourism.

Generally speaking, there is really no dearth of traditional food outlets and tea and snack shops particularly along the highways.

One of the core problems in the study area is lack of *information centers/service*, both in terms of availability and authenticity. By and large, it is also the main reason behind the poor tourist traffic to the Vidarbha Region in particular. Within the study area the tourist information centers are located only at Nagpur and Amravati though one can get some information from the officials of MTDC working at its various accommodation units. There are some information brochures/pamphlets, tourist maps and some CDs have been brought-forth by both Maharashtra Tourism. But most of the time the account provided is incomplete/ patchy not enough to motivate decision-making. Moreover getting these documents itself is difficult on account of the lack of display/ dissemination outlets. Yet another problem is that majority parts of Vidarbh region have yet remained *touristically* lesser studied. As a result, details about meteorological facts, altitude and even distances etc. are either not available/partially available or are based on approximations. It is true both for statistical information and route maps etc. On the whole, provision of effective information and consequently professional marketing requires immediate attention if the region is to judiciously exploit its touristic wealth.

Communication

Good *communication services* are very essential for development of the region. However, the existing state of affairs in the context can hardly be considered satisfactory in the study area. While all the settlements located on roadside and the adjoining villages have now access to *tele-communication* in one or the other form. The fact that presently there are 15 telephone exchanges are functional in eleven districts itself speaks of the situation. As such, tourists travelling along the main approach roads, with some efforts, can use the STD facility.

As regards the *post and telegraph* services, though the available facilities can be rated moderately good. Almost all the major settlements have post offices, while provision of letterboxes maintained by part-time postmen is available even in the remote villages. Likewise, telegraph service is available at all important transit places all along the route.

Bank Services

There are branches of nationalized, cooperative and scheduled banks in the study area, almost evenly distributed in eleven districts. All the destinations and transit places connected with state and national highways have the branches of one or the other bank, which entertain traveller's cheques or bank drafts.

Incidentally, banks at most places do not have currency exchange facility. Likewise, at many places neither the banks nor any other service outlets entertain the credit cards, which are a severe constraint for the travellers, particularly the foreign tourists. Therefore, requisite provisions need to be made at major tourist destinations.

Medical/Healthcare Provisions

The provision of adequate medical facilities yet remains to be one of the extreme constraints in the entire study area, even at the important township located on the roadside leave aside rural areas. As a result traditional ethnic herbal medicinal system is still commonly practiced in the region, though with growing social awareness the once prevalent *superstitious tantra concept of cure* is now steadily vanishing. Though there are many primary health centers in the region, they do not have the requisite stock of even basic medicines. It has also been generally observed that the doctors also avoid their posting in the remoter areas. As a result, the rather ill trained subordinate staff runs these health centers.

Some private practitioners are also found at district headquaters. On the whole, the scenario is far too away from being satisfactory and therefore demands immediate attention.

Drinking Water

There is no dearth of natural water resources in the region, particularly in and around the existing settlements located both enroute and off-route. As such, responsibility of construction part of the water supply schemes rests on *Maharashtra Jal Nigam*, a state level organisation while after completion these schemes are operated and maintained by the *Maharashtra Jal Sansthan* in bigger *Towns* and *Town Area Committees* in smaller Towns. As per the official records, nearby 60 per cent villages and towns in Vidarbha have proper drinking water facilities. At major transit/ tourist center located along the highways of the region MTDC maintain "*Pay Jal units*" (drinking water units) for the convenience of travelling population. However, there is not effective system of appropriate water treatment–though the available water is generally fresh and sweet, but the supply is not proper maintained and the water is not proper treated. Of course, with the popularity of bottled mineral water, the problem of the tourists is temporarily solved, as the same is now available at majority places along the yatra route.

Power Supply

While, all the major settlements located on the main tourist routes are connected with power supply, approximately 75 per cent of villages in Vidarbha now enjoy electricity supply. In view of the ongoing Power Projects in progress in the region, the problem of electricity shortage may not prolong anymore. In fact, on completion of Projects, the state shall be able to sell the excess power to the neighbouring states/national power grid. Meantime *NEDA* (Non-conventional energy development Agency) is consistently trying to set-up series of smaller units at various places to meet the power requirement at micro-level. Unexpected power-cuts do haunt the study area as in any other part of the country. It is particularly disrupted during summer months because of the frequent shortages etc. It may require ample resources in terms of time, money and technology to extend power supply to the villages situated in the remote reaches. It is for this reason that due attention is being paid to popularize the use of solar energy. As such, it is hoped that with grated power production in the region, not only some off-road destinations shall be connected with the power supply, but also more tourist resorts on the lines of Chikhaldara shall be possible to develop.

Percentage of Total Electrified Inhabited Villages Till the Year Mid-2007

S. No.	*Districts*	*Per cent of the Total Villages Connected with Power Supply in Vidarbha*
1.	Akola	8
2.	Amravati	17
3.	Bhandara	10
4.	Buldhana	7
5.	Chandrapur	6
6.	Gadchiroli	2
7.	Gondia	4
8.	Nagpur	22
9.	Wardha	13
10.	Wasim	4
11.	Yavatmal	7

Among various other perspectives safety and security, hygiene and cleanliness, attitude of host population and state of natural environment etc. have vital bearing on the tourism growth potential of a given destination/destination region. Generally speaking, the hill folks are inherently hospitable, honest and cooperative, but not so good on awareness part. Over the years, while the level of awareness has been steadily increasing on account of the better opportunities for communication/interaction with outside world, the growing materialism has started eroding the traditional viewpoint of the people. As such, safety and security or attitude of locals towards the tourists cannot yet be considered as problematic areas, but the former issue needs to be seriously considered, which till date remains virtually unattended. Likewise,

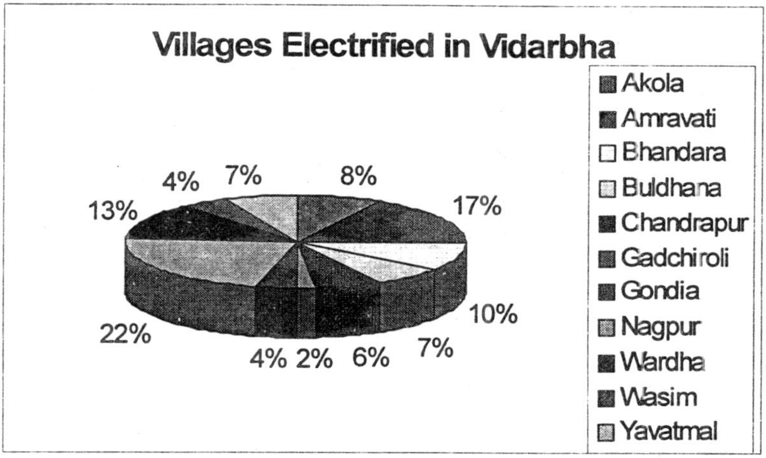

despite the natural setting all around, the problem of cleanliness owing to lack of appropriated waste-disposal system continues to be one of the major problem areas in the relatively larger townships, especially during the pilgrim season. As regards the quality of environment, one can distinctively perceive the fact merely from the fact that larger part of the study area falls in the forested zone. However, over the years, the quality of environment has considerably degraded due to ill-planned developmental activities. Need of the hour is to plan the infrastructural development in a way that it blends with the milieu in a sustained manner.

Recreation and Entertainment

The destination region has, by and large, no such amenities. Indeed, fairs and festivals are celebrated all over the region with great awe and enthusiasm. These occasions, depending on the tradition, may provide glimpses of local folk songs and dances – if a tourist happens to visit the region during festivities. As such, almost every settlement, large or small, has its own traditional fair. In such fairs stage shows called *Tamasha* are held. In fact, *Tamasha* shows are unique to Maharashtra's and Vidarbha's culture and depicts glimpses from either history or the daily life. These are through family entertainers. With careful efforts, the colourful folk dance and music shows can be convened for secular tourists at important transit places.

Shopping Opportunities

Shopping is a vitally significant activity at a destination, both from guest and host viewpoints. For the former, apart from the money, which a souvenir brings in exchange, it gives invaluable publicity to the region and that is why tourist-shopping products are often called as *retrievable tourism products*. Obviously, tourism plays vital role in promotion of local art and craft, which constitute the souvenir items.

The locally produced items like cotton based textiles, toys made out of clay, household and giftable goods made out of bamboo etc. can be excellent souvenir pieces. The hand made textiles made from *Charkha* in Sewagram are especially popular among the tourists. Of late, the exquisite goods made by the physically handicapped people has caught the attention of the tourists.

Tourism Policy of India: An Exploratory Study

Tourism Policy cannot be evolved on its own without being influenced by the general tenor of macro-economic policy. Tourism policy thus has a socio-political grounding as much as it has a macro-economic coloring.

The 1980s witnessed the era of liberalization initiated by the Congress Government at the Centre. The process of liberating the Indian economy from the shibboleths of 'license-permit Raj' culminated in the initiation of the structural adjustment programme in 1992. "Objectives, Thrusts and Macro-economic Dimensions of the Eighth Plan" endorsed by the National Development Council, clearly outlines the context within which the structural reforms were initiated: "The need to restructure our systems of economic management has become an imperative if India is to emerge as a vibrant and internationally competitive economy in the 90's. Systems of control and regulation, developed for good reasons in the past have outlived their utility and some positively stand in the way of further progress. Such dysfunctional systems have to be overhauled in the light of emerging realities.

Any initiative by Government in Tourism by way of legislation or direct investment is envisaged within the framework of Tourism

Policy. The backdrop of a policy always serves as a guideline for further executive and legislative initiatives. It would be cynical to regard these policy statements as mere exercises in eloquence and additions to the already existing volumes of wishful thinking.

Furthermore, Policy statements by Government should be viewed in their evolutionary stance. It would be a negation of the democratic content of our political system to view a Policy statement as a static and rigid formulation, at a point in time, applicable for years to come. Thus, since 1982, various initiatives undertaken by the Government need to be perceived as additions or modifications to the received Policy.

While it may be argued that these changes in the policy are only marginal and superficial from the viewpoint of equity and social justice, it would be an oversimplification to view the latest policy statement as nothing but the "nth" version of the Policy formulated in 1982. Recognising the all-pervading inertia that looms large in matters governmental, one is often tempted to deny the scope for lobbying which makes possible the desired modifications in the policy corpus. In short, policy, as a body incorporating proactive intentions, is amenable to periodic reviews and possible modifications.

Major Policy Initiatives

The first ever Tourism Policy was announced by the Government of India in November 1982. It took ten long years for the Government to feel the need to come up with a possible improvement over this. Thus the National Action Plan for Tourism was announced in May 1992. Between these two policy statements, various legislative and executive measures were brought about. In particular, the report of the National Committee on Tourism, submitted in 1988 needs special mention. In addition, two five-year plans-the Seventh and the Eighth-provided the basic perspective framework for operational initiatives.

The Seventh Plan advocated a two-pronged thrust in the area of development of tourism, viz., to vigorously promote domestic tourism and to diversify overseas tourism in India. While laying stress on creation of beach resorts, conducting of conventions, conferences, winter sports and trekking, the overall intention was to diversify options available for foreign tourists.

The Tourism Policy, 1982 was more an aggressive statement in marketing than a perspective plan for development. Its main thrust was aimed at presenting India to the foreigners as the ultimate holiday resort. With a view to reach this destination, the following measures were suggested by the Policy:

1. To take full advantage of the national heritage in arriving at a popular campaign for attracting tourists;
2. To promote tourist resorts and make India a destination of holiday resorts;
3. To grant the status of an export industry to tourism;
4. To adopt a selective approach to develop few tourist circuits; and,
5. To invite private sector participation into the sector.

The Planning Commission recognised tourism as an industry by June 1982. However, it took ten years to make most of the States to fall in line and accord the same status within their legislative framework. At the beginning of the Eighth Plan (1992-97), 15 States and 3 Union Territories had declared tourism as an industry. Four States had declared hotels as an industry.

The National Committee on Tourism was set up in July 1986 by the Planning Commission to prepare a perspective plan for the sector. Within the broad framework of the Seventh Plan, the Committee had to evolve a perspective plan for the coming years. It suggested that there be a separate cadre of Indian Tourism Service to look after the functioning of the Board. It also submitted proposals for partial privatisation of the two airlines owned by the Union Government.

By September 1987, the Central Government declared more concessions for the sector: these included tax exemption on foreign exchange earnings from tourism (a 50% reduction on rupee earnings and a 100% reduction on earnings in dollars), a drastic reduction in tariff on import of capital goods, and concessional finance at the rate of 1 to 5 per cent per annum.

The Tourism Development Finance Corporation was set up in 1987 with a corpus fund of Rs. 100 crores. Until then, the sector was financed on commercial lines by the Industrial Development Bank of India, Industrial Credit and Investment Corporation of India and other commercial banks.

The National Action Plan for Tourism, published in May 1992, and tabled in the Lok Sabha on 5 May 1992, charts 7 objectives as central concerns of the Ministry:

- Socio-economic development of areas;
- Increasing employment opportunities;
- Developing domestic tourism for the budget category;
- Preserving national heritage and environment;
- Development of international tourism;
- Diversification of the tourism product;
- And, increase in India's share in world tourism (from the present 0.4% to 1% during next 5 years).

As per the Action Plan, foreign exchange earnings were estimated to increase from Rs.10,000 crores in 1992 to Rs. 24,000 crores by 2000 AD. Simultaneously, the Plan aimed at increasing employment in tourism to 28 million from the present 14 million. Hotel accommodation is to be increased from 44,400 rooms to 1,20,000 by 3 years. Other provisions in the Action Plan included a discontinuance of subsidies to star hotels, encouraging foreign investment in tourism and the setting up of a convention city for developing convention tourism.

The Action Plan envisaged the development of Special Tourism Areas on lines of export processing zones. Special Central assistance is to be provided for the States to improve the infrastructural facilities at pilgrimage places. It proposes to set up a National Culinary Institute, and projects a liberalised framework for recognition of travel agents and tour operators.

The Eighth Plan document made a special mention that the future expansion of tourism should be achieved mainly by private sector participation. The thrust areas as enumerated in the Plan include development of selected tourist places, diversification from cultural related tourism to holiday and leisure tourism, development of trekking, winter sports, wildlife and beach resort tourism, exploring new source markets, restoration of national heritage projects, launching of national image building, providing inexpensive accommodation in different tourist centres, improving service efficiency in public sector corporations and streamlining of facilitation procedures at airports.

The Eighth Plan aimed at luring the high spending tourists from Europe and USA. It also envisaged a 'master plan' to integrate area plans with development of tourism. This is envisaged to ensure employment opportunities for the local population.

In April 1993, the Government announced further measures aimed at export promotion. The existing Export Promotion of Capital Goods Scheme (EPCG) was extended to tourism and related services. Against the existing 35 per cent, the tourism sector would now pay an excise duty of 15 per cent only on capital goods import, subject to an export obligation of 4 times the cargo, insurance and freight (CIF) value of imports. With an obligation period of five years, this came as a boon to the hotel industry. The cost of construction had also come down by 20 per cent.

In addition to the above policy pronouncements by the Union Government, our planners had envisaged the possibilities of developing specific regions on a zonal plank. Special area programmes like the Hill Area Development Programme and the Western Ghats Development Programme form part of the overall national plan.

The Eighth Plan document stipulates that the strategy in such designated special areas is to devise suitable location-specific solutions, so as to reverse the process of degradation of natural resources and ensure sustainable development. This approach perhaps needs to be integrated into the project of special tourism areas, now being made popular by the Government. Administrative Control and Developmental Compromises. Seventeen circuits and destinations were identified under the National Action Plan for development through Central assistance and investment by the States and the private sector.

NATIONAL TOURISM POLICY 2002

Salient Features

Mission

The National Tourism Policy 2002 emphasized that tourism would lead to larger foreign exchange earnings and create conditions for more Foreign Direct Investment.

The mission statement of policy was to promote sustainable tourism as a means of economic growth and social integration and to promote the image of India abroad as a country with a glorious past, a vibrant present and a bright future. Policies to achieve this will be evolved around six broad areas such as Welcome (swagat), Information (suchana), Facilitation (suvidha), Safety (suraksha), Cooperation (Sahyog) and Infrastructure Development (Samrachana). Conservation of heritage, natural environments, etc., and *development and promotion of tourist products would also be given importance.*

Role of the Government, Private Sector and their Partnership

While the primary role of the government, according to the policy, is to provide basic infrastructural facilities including local planning and zoning arrangements, the primary role of private sector is to build and manage the required tourist facilities in all places of tourist interest. However greater emphasis was give to the partnership between them. Apart form this the role of voluntary agencies and volunteers, who contribute their expertise and understanding of local ethos to supplement the efforts of other sectors to provide the human touch to tourism and foster local initiatives, will also be recognized.

Funds

It would be the policy of the Government to facilitate larger flow of funds to tourism infrastructure and to create a Tourism Development Fund to bridge critical infrastructure gaps.

Foreign Investments and Incentives and Rationalization of Taxes

(a) In view of large investment requirements in the tourism sector and the need for maintaining high quality standards

in services, hotels and tourism related industries will continue to be in the priority list of industries for foreign investment. Export-house status has been accorded to Hotels, Travel Agents, Tour Operators and Tourist Transport Operators vide Notification No. 33 (RE-98)1997-2002 dated 26.11.98 of the Ministry of Commerce. The status needs to be extended to all tourism units irrespective of the annual turnover.

(b) In order to offset the specific constraints of tourism industry and to put in place the required infrastructure as quickly as possible, particularly in less developed areas, appropriate incentive schemes would be considered. It would also be the endeavour of the Government to persuade the State/UT Governments to rationalize taxes, to put a cap of 20 per cent on all taxes taken together on the accommodation and hospitality units, to allocate suitable land for tourism purposes at reasonable prices, harmonize movement of tourist transport across State borders, etc.

Adoption of New Technologies

Efforts will be made to adopt the technological advances in the tourism sector to provide better facilities to tourists and to market the tourism product, to the benefit of all concerned.

Safety and Security

The safety and security of tourists are of primary importance both from the point of view of tourism development and the national pride. It will be, therefore, given high priority in the national strategy for tourism development. Central Government will take up with the State Government to enact suitable legislation on travel trade/tourist police for protection and security of tourists and for providing institutional mechanism to deal with complaints received from tourists and the industry so as to create a better security perception amongst actual and potential visitors.

Placing Tourism in the Concurrent List of the Constitution of India

Tourism as a separate subject does not find a place in the Seventh Schedule of the Constitution of India even though a number of its components are either in the Union List or in the State List or in the Concurrent List. Under the new Policy, Tourism will be placed in the Concurrent List as such a step will provide a Constitutional recognition to the tourism sector and help in channelising development of tourism in a systematic manner by enabling the Central Government to bring in legislation governing the activities of various service providers in the tourism sector.

Other Salient Features

- Development of Tourism Economic Zone, Tourist Circuits, Special Tourism Area and Areas of Special Interests
- Sustainable Development and Perspective Plans
- Conservation and Development
- Promotions and Marketing
- International Co-operation
- Professional Excellence.

EVALUATION OF NATIONAL TOURISM POLICY

Undoubtedly, looking at its multiple benefits, governments simply cannot ignore tourism activities and the current tourism policy is a step in the right direction. However, as seen in the past, policy implementation is far behind the policy formation. Many of the excellent ideas in the past have remained on pen and paper for the want of sufficient attention and funds.

STATE TOURISM POLICY DRAFT – MAHARASHTRA

Located on the western coast of India abutting the Arabian Sea lies Maharashtra. Replete with virgin beaches, exotic wildlife, verdant hills, quaint hill stations, scenic villages, coastal forts, caves and cave temples, there is much more to Maharashtra than meets the eye. Apart from the few destinations which have been high on the popularity charts to the extent of being over-exposed, there are several other interesting regions waiting to take centre stage.

Treading the Eco-Trail

Realising the potential of eco-tourism as a revenue maker for the state, tourist attractions ranging from forts, caves, hill stations, beaches, pilgrimage centres, forest reserves and wildlife sanctuaries are being developed keeping ecological considerations in mind.

The conservation and development around the world heritage sites, Ajanta and Ellora, follows the principles of eco-tourism. Maharashtra is aggressively marketing itself as a premier global eco-tourism destination. The state tourism board with the help of the State Government and NGOs has initiated special eco-tourism ventures to develop and promote the eco-potential of the state to an international clientele.

Focus on Ajanta-Ellora

The state has demarcated regions to promote the concept of eco-tourism in the region. Eco-tourism ventures have been introduced in areas such as Vidarbha, Sawantwadi, Aurangabad etc. Wildlife protection, nature conservation activities, monument upgradation, heritage property restoration, fort improvement and protection are all part of the state's eco-tourism initiative. One of the most prominent initiative has been at the Ajanta Ellora site in Aurangabad where a number of programmes have been instituted with eco-tourism as the primary focus. The caves are world heritage monuments, which contain paintings and carvings dating back to 200 BC. These monuments attract more than a million tourists every year and are one of the most important tourist destinations in India. The Ajanta caves are about 100 kms from Aurangabad, which acts as the main gateway for the tourists visiting the area. Aurangabad is a well-developed town with industry, commerce and tourism as its principal source of revenue generation. The area has a very large number of tourist attractions comprising ancient caves, outstanding forts, a mausoleum similar to Taj Mahal, museums, unique handicraft industry etc.

The first phase of restoration work undertaken at the Ajanta Ellora caves is a classic example in which Maharashtra Tourism Development Corporation (MTDC) submitted a plan for restoration of the area in and around the two heritage sites to the Government of India. This proposal was then submitted to the Government of Japan. The Japanese Bank of International Cooperation and the Government of Maharashtra jointly funded the restoration plan.

Detailed scientific investigations were carried out by the Geological Survey of India at Ajanta and Ellora caves and based on their report a site management plan which included conservation, was carried out. The conservation work included protection of the rock mass, prevention of water seepage, slope stability, surface water management, landscaping of the adjoining region and development of a circulation plan. The conservation work being carried out at the caves has set standards in cave protection and visitor management system for ancient monuments in the country.

A scenic pathway from the Ajanta viewpoint to the foot of caves was planned which provides a panoramic view of caves to visitors. The afforestation work of Phase I was started immediately after signing the loan agreement and afforestation of about 180 hectares of forest was carried out by the first year and the remaining portion of 737 hectares was taken up for afforestation in the next two seasons. Afforestation has provided the following benefits:

- Forest walkways and nature walks.
- Improved vegetation cover, which will prevent the soil erosion highly prevalent in the area.
- Provision of leisure and picnicking places to tourists near the monuments.
- Bringing down the NO, CO_2, and dust particle counts much below the permissible limits.
- Raising the ground water level. Roads leading to the Ajanta and Ellora caves from Aurangabad, which is the main gateway for tourism activities in the region, were improved. Improvement of some small roads surrounding the caves was also included. The improvement of these roads resulted in a drastic reduction of vehicular population near Ellora caves and smooth and easy flow of tourist traffic from Aurangabad to Ajanta (15 kms) and Ellora (25 kms).
- Two lane roads for all tourist destinations in the region.
- Black topped roads in the Ellora caves complex for ease of vehicular movement. International grade highway and direction signage.

The water supply scheme for the cave areas and the tourist complexes will be developed in Phase II. The water sources for Ajanta and Ellora are the Tondapur dam and Khultabad water system respectively. The benefits from the scheme are as follows:

- Availability of water of international hygiene standard
- Adequate water supply catered for tourist traffic till 2020
- Water supply available for maintaining the landscaping and gardens
- There will be no open drainage which would impinge on the hygiene of the area near the monuments.

The package was planned to supply power to the tourist complexes and caves. For Ajanta, upgrading the Fardapur sub-station and installation of transmission lines from Pahur sub-station with 20.5 km length was based on the power demand of 6394 kw. For Ellora, upgrading the Ellora sub-station and installation of transmission line from Khultabad sub-station to Ellora and Daulatabad with a total length of 28 kms was based on the estimated demand of 860 km. At both the sites the existing sub-stations were augmented with additional power transformers and associated control switch gear.

In a bid to protect the world heritage site, (MTDC) has introduced special, pollution free luxury buses (5 AC and 5 Non-AC) on the 2.5 kms along stretch of the Ajanta tour that begins at Fardapur. The MTDC authorities have also banned the use of all other vehicles in the area. The entire exercise is expected to reduce the vehicular traffic and pollution in the surrounding areas of the Ajanta caves. No vehicles are allowed to park near the caves making the entire surrounding area eco-friendly and pollution free.

The monument conservation programme practiced at Ajanta Ellora would also be carried out at other similar sites with time. Karla, Elephanta etc. would be part of this initiative.

Greener Pastures

The state government in a bid to concentrate effectively on eco-tourism, heritage and convention centers has invited private participation from both domestic and foreign investors.

In the same vein, the Forest Development Corporation of Maharashtra (FDCM) Ltd., has appointed the Indian Society for Environment, Art and Cultural Heritage (Indsearch) to conduct eco-tours in the vicinity of the forests in Maharashtra. There is excellent potential for eco-tourism since Maharashtra has an estimated forest cover of more than 103 square kilometers. The FDCM along with the forest department of Maharashtra plans to utilize the existing available infrastructure for the development of eco-tourism along with Indsearch, who will conduct guided tours in various forests, sanctuaries and wildlife areas besides organising nature camps, rural tours, outdoor management development programmes for the corporate sector.

Packaging Adventure and the Wild West

The Sahyadri range offers plenty of opportunity for trekking, hiking and rock climbing. There are a number of interesting mountain-top forts, a window to the hey-day of the reign of the Marathas, part of the rich historical legacy of the state. MTDC has taken steps for the promotion of adventure and wildlife tourism in the state, especially in the Nagpur belt. It has joined hands with the neighbouring Madhya Pradesh Government towards the same. Madhya Pradesh (MP) is the leading state as far as wildlife tourism is concerned. Though Kanha and Bandhavgarh tiger sanctuaries in MP are world renowned, Maharashtra has Tadoba and Melghat which are bigger tiger sanctuaries but they have not been developed and marketed strongly. There are many other sanctuaries and pockets of thickly forested areas in the state which could be developed and promoted as adventure and wildlife tourism zones.

A jungle lodge has been developed by MTDC at Tadoba, close to Nagpur. The entire ambience there is in tune with the spirit of nature and it's a conscious effort on the part of MTDC to move on to the path of wildlife tourism.

Scaling New Heights With Fort Tourism

MTDC has set out a plan to promote fort tourism in the state. Various forts, especially in the western Maharashtra region, which were built and used by Shivaji, have been identified as prospective areas of interest for tourism. The proposal of drafting a special fort itinerary which will be spread over a period of approximately 15 days is on the anvil. Provisions in the nature of professionals and experts with a specific guided plan along with identified accommodation area will be offered. Fort conservation and protection plans are also being conceptualised by some local NGOs in the region.

Hill Stations

The state has a diverse spread of natural attractions, fauna and flora. The 720 kms long Konkan coastal strip extends eastwards from its estuaries and mangroves, across the majestic mountain ranges of the western ghats and 900 kms inland to the dry, deciduous zones of Vidarbha. The Sahyadri range, a part of these ghats is clothed in evergreen deciduous forests. These picturesque mountain ranges are among the oldest in the world. The Saputara hills along the northern border and the Bhamragad-Chiroli-Gaikhuri ranges along the east, serve as natural limits to the state and still remain virgin as a tourism offering. These hills and mountain ranges offer a number of challenging trekking trails and house abundant wildlife.

The state has some wonderful hill stations. Unfortunately only a few have been really developed and publicised while the rest are languishing in obscurity. Amongst the more popular hill stations are Matheran, Mahabaleshwar and Lonavala, whilst Amboli near Sawantwadi on the Goa border, Malshej ghat near Mumbai and Panhala near Kolhapur are relatively unexplored hill retreats. Chikaldhara, another pristine hill station has not been fully exploited due to its geographic distance from the Mumbai, the gateway to Maharashtra. This destination houses the Pench Tiger Reserve.

Hill Station Protection Plan

Matheran and Mahabaleshwar, two of the most well known and highly populous hill stations of Maharashtra have been facing severe environmental abuse due to too much human interface. Though Matheran has been protected with a ban on vehicular traffic in the region, ruthless cutting down of trees have led to a total ecological disturbance in the hill station. The Supreme Court of India has declared both the hill stations as eco-friendly zones and all constructions in the area have been put on an indefinite standstill to protect the region from further environmental damage.

Rural and Beach Initiatives

The state has also introduced 'rustic valley tours' in the area close to Lonavala with the help of an NGO. The focus is to stimulate and help sustainable local women's enterprises in the tourism sector, in keeping with the local culture and natural environment. Educating the visitors on nature, tradition, agriculture, rural development etc. is part of the village tourism promotion plan.

Meanwhile, the Sawantwadi Eco Tourism Plan also emphasises on developing Sawantwadi as a complete eco-tourism zone. Efforts have been taken by the Sawantwadi municipal council, along with the support of Rachana Sansad's Institute of Environmental Architecture, Government of Maharashtra and MTDC to develop Sawantwadi region as a primary eco zone. The aim is to make the entire Sindhudurg district an eco village and eco-tourism centre. The local arts and crafts will be promoted. Ganjifa playing cards and wooden furniture which are painted by natural watercolours made up of different variety of soils, mud and leaves, which is the region's speciality, is being promoted. Eco-friendly technology is being incorporated to promote this kind of art. An arts and craft village, Shipagram, is yet another concept which is being developed.

Tarkarli has already evolved as a major destination in the district with Maharashtra Tourism Development Corporation (MTDC) setting up a beachfront resort with Konkani style cottages. A new concept of 'houseboat' on the sands with two suites has been introduced. The famous sea fort of Sindhudurg, off the Malvan coast close-by, is a big attraction besides the casurina-lined Tarkarli beach. International cruise liners operating in Indian waters have included Tarkarli as a day-long excursion in their itinerary.

The tourist resort at Ganapatipule, run by Maharashtra tourism, has built Konkani huts so that the tourist gets a taste of the local flavour in accommodation. Another exciting concept introduced by the tourism department is 'Village Tourism' in Hadi.

Environment Awareness and Nature Interpretation Centres

In regions that are thick in flora and fauna, predominantly forests and hills, environment awareness and natural interpretation centres are planned to be set up to study ecological diversities in the region. These centres would cater to the needs of special interest groups such as environmentalists, nature activists, students, locals and others. Vidarbha area, which has around 27 wildlife sanctuaries, four national parks along with promising routes for trekking, nature trails etc. would be one of the areas for setting up such a centre. Nature interpretation centres will help provide information about flora and fauna in the region through posters and audio-visuals. A herbarium for medicinal plants, a lepidoptera or a butterfly zoo as well as a mini planetarium for star-gazing would be part of the centre at Sawantwadi. The centre will also serve as a demonstration centre for eco-friendly construction technologies as well as for renewable energy, watershed management, water and waste recycling. In the Narendra hills area which is rich in natural fauna and flora, specialised nature trials would be organised by the members of Sawantwadi Eco Development Council with the support of NGOs along with the forest department. The region will have a centre called the Nishi Fondge Environment Awareness Centre which will exhibit photographs and information regarding wildlife in and around Sawantwadi.

Amboli which is an evergreen forest and a place that receives the second highest rainfall in India has been identified as a region for undertaking special eco-tourism initiatives. Tadoba, Navegaon National Park, regions in the Sahyadris etc. have also been marked for setting up of such centres.

Lonar Crater

Once upon a time, not very far from Mumbai, a great big chunk of a meteor hurtled down and struck the earth. It is today known to have formed the world's oldest crater on the outskirts of Lonar town in district Buldhana in Maharashtra. This is the only crater in the world created by hypervelocity meteoric impact in basaltic rock. MTDC realised the potential of this crater and has aggressively been promoting Lonar as a major tourist destination. To this end they also set up a 'Crater View Tourist Complex', overlooking the depression in the earth. The crater which is a green depression, perfectly circular and 1.8 km in diameter, is in the middle of a vast plain of parched fields and riverbeds. At the bottom of this grotesquely large bowl lies a still emerald lake. The lake has a high concentration of salt, explaining the absence of fish, and a perennial stream keeps its level constant even in the monsoons. This crater has been attracting international tourists and scientists. The lake is the third largest salt-water lake in the world. Due to its very nature, the region has attracted specialised eco initiatives unique only to Lonar. MTDC is in the process of conducting studies about activities in the region due to the formation of the crater.

New Offerings

The state's 720 kms long coastline has remained relatively undiscovered and unexploited compared to states like Goa and Kerala. Sindhudurg district, which was declared by the Maharashtra Government as a 'Tourism District', has some of the best beaches in the state and country. Kunkeshwar, Tarkarli, Deobagh, Vengurla, Mochemad, Shiroda are some of the scenic beaches dotting the coastline of the district. Eco tourism drives and initiatives are being planned along the coastline area. Ganpatipule with the Swayambhoo Ganpati temple on the beach and Bhatye beach in Ratnagiri have also developed as major beach destinations. Others up north like Harihareshwar, Murud Janjira, Kihim, Alibag are already popular while there are a number of other beaches like Murud-Harnai, Velneshwar etc. which have remained relatively undiscovered due to lack of accommodation. NGO's have been active in preserving marine life across the coastal belt of the state. Environment friendly measures are being incorporated to preserve the beaches in the regions.

Traversing The Eco-Trail on The Deccan Odyssey

Promising to take tourists on a journey through a kaleidoscope land and an experience rich with exotic and diverse images, a 'Pan Maharashtra' luxury train–The Deccan Odyssey–is on the anvil for which a Memorandum of Understanding has already been signed with the railways. From pristine beaches, to defiant forts, from stories and Gods carved in black monolithic rock, to opulent palaces dedicated to kings, from north to south and one century to another, this luxury train offers to take its passengers on a journey through the kingdom of the Marathas, Maharashtra.

Characterised by luxury, The Deccan Odyssey will sport ten stately theme suites. Facilities and services aboard this luxury train include two tastefully designed lounge and conference cars allowing passengers to mix business with pleasure. Other features comprise of a specialty restaurant, to match the finest India has to offer and an exceptionally well-stocked bar, to contribute to the entire experience of luxury. Passengers will also be able to enjoy on demand–Foreign Exchange facility on board. The eight day itinerary includes several exotic destinations covering the expanse of Maharashtra.

This venture stands to enhance the tourism potential of Maharashtra, being developed on the lines of the Orient Express, by the Integral Coach Factory, Chennai. This 21-coach luxury train will also set a trend in rail conferencing, a new and innovative break through in the field of corporate conferencing.

However, there is a lot more to look out for on board–a gym, beauty shop, yoga centre and ayurvedic treatments. There would also be two restaurants cum kitchen cars that would serve varied local authentic and continental cuisine. A unique feature about the conference coach is that it is designed in a way that it could also be converted into a disco-cum-pub for evening entertainment. MTDC has planned an aggressive marketing campaign and will be show-casing the luxury train in upcoming travel marts abroad.

The train aims to showcase the state's art, culture and heritage. Development of the Konkan coast on the lines of the French Riviera are new concepts that have been strategised. Promotion of Vipasana and Ayurveda tours, especially at the Vipasana Kendra at Igatpuri near Nashik will be aggressively done to meet the international demand for both the products. Participation in tourism fairs, both national and international, has thus been high on the agenda of the state's promotional drives.

Evaluation of State Tourism Policy

As can be seen from the above tourism policy draft of Maharashtra the focus is on Eco-tourism, Adventure and wildlife, fort, hill station, nature interpretation centers and rural initiative. Fortunately, Vidarbha has just the right combination of all these elements. The vast stretch of forest has ample scope for Adventure and wildlife and Eco-tourism. Vidarbha can boast of Chikhaldara hill station and Gavilgarh fort. The presence of many tribal settlements in the region can fulfill the rural initiative. There is already a nature interpretation center at Melghat and the same can be done for the other national parks and wildlife sanctuaries in the region. But the policy has little or nothing for Vidarbha region. Even the special tourist train "Deccan Odyssey" does not touch Vidarbha region. Clearly what follows is a comparative study of the state of Tourist Development between Maharashtra (Mumbai Side) and Vidharbha (Nagpur Side). The only consolation is the mention of Lonar Crator in the policy document. Another encouraging feature is the mention of Tourism Development of Vidarbha region in the budget speech of 2003-04 and 2004-05. The same part has been reproduced below as it is:

*"Large areas of **Vidharbha** are under forest cover and the region is well suited for the development of wildlife and eco-tourism. It is proposed to develop special wildlife tourism zones with strong private sector participation. The Maharashtra Tourism Development Corporation will acquire land outside the wildlife sanctuaries and offer it for development. A provision of Rs. 5 crore has been proposed for the year 2003-04 for this purpose. The development of wildlife eco-tourism in Vidarbha will contribute significantly to employment generation in the tribal dominated forest areas of Vidarbha. The conservation of the meteorite impact centre of Lonar in Buldhana district will be taken up with a view to preserving this fragile and unique eco-system and developing it as a world tourist destination".*

COMPARATIVE STUDY OF THE STATE OF TOURIST DEVELOPMENT BETWEEN MAHARASHTRA (MUMBAI SIDE) AND VIDHARBHA (NAGPUR SIDE)

Allocation of Funds for Removal of Backlog

Government had appointed a Fact Finding Committee (FFC) in August 1983 to assess the regional backlog in various sectors of development and to suggest measures to remove the same. The FFC submitted its report in June 1984, in which it had worked out a backlog of Rs. 3,186.78 crores.

SWOT ANALYSIS OF TOURIST POTENTIAL IN VIDARBHA

Strengths

1. Strategic Location: Mid-way from metros. Can be promoted as break-journey/ stop-over destination.
2. Abundant natural scenic beauty and wildlife.
3. Amalgamation of tribal and modern culture.
4. Places historical importance and archaeological remains.

Weaknesses

1. Poor policy framework
2. Poor infrastructure
3. Extreme weather
4. Lack of awareness and marketing efforts.

Opportunities

1. Eco-tourism
2. Adventure Tourism
3. Rural and Ethnic Tourism
4. Employment and Foreign Exchange.

Threats

1. Cultural Erosion
2. Poaching/Timber logging
3. Naxal Movement
4. Declining water level.

Strengths

Vidarbha has many inherent strengths of its own. First is its strategic central location. Being equidistant from all the four metropolitan cities of the country it has the potential to become a super travel and tourism hub. Therefore it can really be promoted as a stop-over destinations while visiting Golden Triangle in the north and backwaters in the south.

Nature has gifted Vidarbha with its bounties like nowhere else. Thus nature-based tourism can work wonders for Vidarbha like it has done for Kerala or Chhattisgarh. Moreover, the very life in Vidarbha is an amalgamation of tribal and modern culture that can be positioned as a unique tourism product. On the top of it, there is no dearth of places of tourist interest in Vidarbha coupled with sites of archeological remains.

Weaknesses

However, there are weaknesses too. There's no proper policy framework by the either the Central or State Government to develop tourism in this region. This coupled with poor infrastructure puts Vidarbha way behind the other regions. The central location away from the coasts has got its disadvantages too. The weather is quite extreme leaving considerably less time suitable for tourism operations. What bothers more is the lack of awareness among the local people. They need to develop the receptive attitude towards the foreign visitor and welcome them with a smile. Moreover, due to lack of marketing efforts, many of the potential visitors are not aware of what Vidarbha has to offer. A proper marketing strategy coupled with information dissemination centers can do wonders for tourism in Vidarbha.

Opportunities

Opportunities for tourism activities are just galore at Vidarbha. You name it, and Vidarbha has it! While the vast stretch of green provides ample scope for eco-tourism, the rugged landscape is just right for adventure activities. The other aspect that can be cashed upon is the rural and ethnic tourism. A number of tribal settlements exists in the Vidarbha region that can draw the attention of the visitor who would like to experience the life of these people which has seldom changed in the last thousand years. All these activities can bring in the much-desired foreign exchange and also provide employment to millions.

Threats

The main threat to Vidarbha is the depletion of the forest covers. As discussed earlier the vast green is one of the major strengths of Vidarbha. Therefore, large scale timber logging and poaching of the wild animals posing a major threat to Vidarbha region. Apart from these the naxal movements in some parts brings in the safety issues to the forefront and also hinders the tourist movement. There is a considerable fear that when the tribal people come much in contact with the visitor it might lead to cultural erosion. They might start imitating the visitors and forget their own culture. Another alarming trend is the declining water level of the region. As water is the very basis to life at any place the scarcity of water might change the biotic and abiotic life of the region.

5

Strategy for Tourism Promotion in Vidarbha Region

IDENTIFICATION OF PRIORITY MARKET

India's tourism industry is booming due to a rush of foreign tourists and increased travel by Indians to domestic and overseas destinations. The visitors are pouring in from all over the world: Europe, Africa, Southeast Asia and Australia. At the same time, the number of Indians travelling abroad last year increased by 30 per cent, to 4.5 million. The boom has come even as global tourism has dropped, due to the September 11 terrorist attacks in the United States, the outbreak of Severe Acute Respiratory Syndrome in East Asia, and the Iraq war.

Tourism professionals cite several reasons for the buoyancy in the Indian industry. The recent surge in the Indian economy has raised middle class incomes, prompting more people to spend money on vacations abroad or at home. At the same time, India's emergence as a global information technology hub and an aggressive advertising campaign by the government are credited with changing India's image from that of a land of snake-charmers, and sparking new interest among overseas travellers.

The world's leading travel publication, the Lonely Planet, last year listed India as one of the five top "must-see" destinations for global leisure travellers.

Earlier it was a winter industry, but now even in the so-called lean summer and rainy seasons tourists are pouring in. Some of them are from Middle East countries. They come to witness the drenching monsoon rains in India, a phenomenon never seen in desert climates.

Domestic tourists are also fueling the industry's revival. Many of them escape from the summer heat on the plains to resorts in the Himalayan Mountains. One of the major beneficiaries this year is Kashmir, where a cease-fire between India and Pakistan has reduced violence, if not completely, at least enough to help revive the state's sagging tourism industry.

According to the market research done by WTO, Western Europe and the USA is the main tourist generating regions for India. But most of them end up doing the Golden Triangle (Delhi, Agra, Jaipur) in the north and of late, Kerala down south. Clearly, Vidarbha is a neglected part in between. Thus, in the beginning, Vidarbha must consider these cash rich countries as its priority market and focus on projecting itself as an extension of a golden triangle itinerary or south India itinerary.

Vidarbha can adopt a two-pronged strategy for its promotion. On the one hand, it must do an aggressive marketing campaign at the tourist generating regions. This will generate more queries about the region and information kiosks at convenient locations can convert these queries into business. On the other, it must persuade the local inbound tour operators at the gateways to India, namely Delhi and Mumbai, to suggest Vidarbha to their clients. With discreet incentive they can be lured into the business.

Infrastructure Development

Infrastructure is the lifeline of tourism industry. As discussed in the previous chapter it includes the *three 'A's* namely, *Accessibility*, *Accommodation* and the *Amenities*. Many destinations of Vidarbha with tourism potential lie neglected for the want of accessibility. At some places there is not even a motorable road and the visitor have to walk miles for the destination. Similarly the central location of Nagpur and its equidistance from the metros can make it a super railway hub. Indian Railways can be a partner in the promotion of tourism circuits in the Vidarbha region. Besides the surface transport aviation needs to be developed in the region. Besides making Nagpur an international airport, the airstrips at

Amravati and Akola can be developed into full-fledged airports. Even the helicopter services are recommended for far off places like Chandrapur and Gadchiroli.

Similarly there is an acute shortage of accommodation units in Vidarbha. While the private entrepreneurs are shy to invest, the MTDC has accommodation units at selected places. In the previous chapter a table gives the number of beds available at each location. The amenities at a destination are equally important to draw tourists. These include telecom and broadband facilities, banking and exchange facilities, wayside amenities etc. These are in its nascent stage in Vidarbha and needs to be taken care of urgently.

Peoples Involvement, Training and Awareness

For the success of any tourist destination the guest-host relationship is very important. Though the people of Vidarbha are in general very hospitable, yet there is a need to create awareness about tourism and at the same time seek their participation in the development of tourism industry. A service industry like tourism needs highly professional people. Hiring people from other regions or the metros may be costly and thus Vidarbha must have a state-of-the-art institute to train its manpower and utilize their services. Therefore the existing universities can diversify to include tourism in their curriculum.

Promotional Strategies

Enthralled by its beauty and the culture, many foreign tourist want to visit India. But they also have their reservations like health concerns, difficult living conditions, and poverty. It's an image India–one of the world's fastest-growing economies, and a nuclear power eager for a permanent seat in the United Nations Security Council–wants to shake off. Going on a major makeover offensive, the country jacked up its tourism budget from Rs. 500 crore ($116.3 million) in 2003 to Rs.786 crore ($182.79 million) in 2004.

Indian President Abdul Kalam has set the country a target of luring 15 million foreign tourists per year in five years–an ambitious jump from the 3.7 million visitors India welcomes each year. If

Vidarbha has to take its pie from this it must harp on an aggressive promotional campaign. Some of the promotional strategies are discussed below.

Brochures

Brochures are the basic promotional literature that every tourism organization uses. However if Vidarbha has to make a mark, it has to be different. The promotional literature has to be of high quality with modern outlook. It has to have easy lay out, accurate data and supported by interesting pictographic maps. Sufficient brochures must be distributed to agents abroad and inbound tour operators in India. Thematic brochures on the following themes are recommended:

1. Arts and Crafts
2. Adventure Sports
3. Shopping
4. Fairs and Festivals
5. Dance and Music
6. Body, Mind and Soul
7. Nature and Wildlife
8. Pilgrimages
9. Museums and Art Galleries
10. Things to Do

Two model brochures are given below:

Model–I

10 Must Things to do at Vidarbha:

1. Steal Some Quiet Moments at Chikhaldara

Chikahaldara is a quiet hill station that yet to be commercially exploited. So if someone wants to spend a few quiet moments with his nears and dears, this is just the right place.

2. Visit the Nature's Wonder – Lonar

Lonar is a nature's wonder that will create equal enthusiasm among a casual visitor as well as a geomorphology scholar. Its similarity with the rocks of the planet Mars will definitely bring in more scholars.

3. *Visit an Orange Orchard*

One of the most spectacular sights is the ripened orange in the orchards. Vidarbha's orange is famous both for its size and taste. So just visit an orchard and savor the mouth watering oranges.

4. *Attend a Nature Orientation Camp at Melghat*

A nature orientation camp is an opportunity to understand our Mother Earth and the need to save it in its pristine form to our next generation. Given the environment depletion worldwide attending such nature interpretation camps are a necessity.

5. *Dance to the Tune of Tribal Music*

Tribal music is a welcome change to the urban people who are used to the blaring electronic instrument. The soothing music of simple natural instruments coupled with the unique sounds of the jungle is a different experience altogether.

6. *Know the Culture of the Dwindling Parsi Community*

The number of Parsi community is fast declining. With that the very culture of the Parsis too is becoming rare. However the Parsis are charming hosts and one must get the feel of their culture before this community becomes extinct.

7. *Taste Varhadi Cuisine*

A visit to Vidarbha is incomplete without tasting its cuisine. It has something for everybody. For those who have a sweet tooth there is Puranpoli, Shrikhand, Basundhi. For those who like it hot and spicy, Varhadi Mutton is worth giving a try.

8. *Spend a Day at Baba Amte's Anand Van*

Anand Van is a place set up and run by those afflicted by Leprosy disease. The smooth management of this place is living symbol of 'simple living, high thinking'. A visit to this place has inspired many to take up the cause of selfless service to the humanity.

9. *Spot the Tigers at Tadoba and Pench*

Spotting a tiger in the wild is a different experience altogether than watching it in a zoo or a circus. The thrill associated with it is just inexpressible. One has to see it to believe it. Given the vast area of nature cover in Vidarbha, spotting a tiger in the wild s much easier. It will never disappoint any tourist.

10. Watch the Birds at Lakes in Bhandara

Bhandara, the land of thousand lakes, is a bird watcher's paradise. In the winters migratory birds from as far as Siberia visit these wetlands. Thus this place is of equal importance for the amateur visitor as well as professional scholars.

Model - II

A to Z of Vidarbha (26 Jewels of Vidarbha):

A: Ancient Heritage

The history of Vidarbha is as old as Indian Civilization itself. Since it has been the part of the great epic Ramayana and Mahabharata, it has been it the folklores from time immemorial. One more interesting feature of Vidarbha is that it has written records of past 900 years. No other region of Maharashtra matches this feat.

B: Bison

One of the endangered species.

C: Chikhaldara

Quiet Hill Station

D: Dinosaur egg

Fossils of the giant dinosaurs and their eggs

E: Education

F: Flying squirrel

An animal unique to the forest of Vidarbha

G: Ganesh Festival

The grand gala 10-days festival of Lord Ganesh

H: Hemalkasa

The first and only orphanage of wild animals

I: Ideally Located

Central India location

J: Jungles

Jungles dense enough to give you a feel of night even in broad daylight

K: Korku

The largest tribal community

L: Lonar

The only impact crator in basaltic rock in world

M: Migratory Birds Watching Paradise

Bhandara, the land of thousand lake invites migratory bird from as far as Siberia

N: Naturopathy

Physical well being using the natural resources

O: Oranges

The best quality of Oranges in India

P: Puran Poli

Mouth watering Sweet Pan-cake

Q: Quaint Forts

Gavilgad, Narnala, Ambagarh.

R: Rangoli

The colourful art found on doorsteps.

S: Sevagram

Where Gandhiji, the apostle of peace taught simplicity and truth

T: Tigers

The largest concentration of royal Bengal tigers in the forests of Vidarbha.

U: Underground Temple Treasures

Temples having underground tunnels at Salbardi, Kaundanyapur.

V: Varhadi Mutton

The hot and spicy non-vegetarian cuisine

W: Wildlife

Anoundance of wildlife in the forests of Vidarbha.

X: Xanadu (Beautiful Place)

Serene and beautiful natural places at Gadhchiroli

Y: Yoga

The ancient Indian science of mind, body and soul

Z: Zunka bhakar

A common bread and pulse specialty.

Multimedia Presentation (CD-ROMs)

After India's stupendous success in information technology revolution, both national and state tourism organizations have been making use of multimedia presentation to woo the tourists. In the western countries virtually every household has a personal computer. Thus presenting them Vidarbha in the electronic CD-ROM format will have its own inherent advantages. First, a single CD-ROM of a few grams can contain information of loads of printed brochures and thus it is very handy. Secondly, since it can contain moving images the prospective visitors can take a virtual tour of the destination. To make it more interesting and active these CDs can be made in an interactive format. These CD-ROMs again can either represent whole of Vidarbha or just take one of the above theme at a time. But it must have high resolution quality images, user friendly and easily navigable. These CDs can be distributed to the local in bound operators who in turn can make presentation to their principal agents abroad. Also it can be placed in Indian embassies/missions as well as tourist offices abroad from where the prospective clients can easily pick up.

Print and Electronic Advertisement

We are now in a world in which all goods and services are advertised in both print and electronic media as a part of aggressive marketing campaign. Vidarbha too must advertise its destinations in leading dailies, radio and television programmes both in India and abroad. If a person reads about Vidarbha in morning newspaper, sees a billboard about it on his way to the office, hear about it on the local FM radio on his way back and finally watches about it in the evening soap operas on TV, he is at least bound to make a query. Now it will be our turn to make this query into business. The advertisement must have images of exotic locales so that it stays in the memory of a person long after he saw it. The only hitch is that while advertising abroad careful selection of the print dailies or weeklies as well as the programmes of radio and televisions are to be made.

Fam Tours

Familiarization tours, or Fam Tours in short, are the trips organized by the host destination for the stakeholders of the business. Vidarbha need to organize such fam tours for the foreign outbound operators and Indian inbound operators. These fam tours must give them a taste of everything about Vidarbha. Such fam tours will give them a first hand experience of Vidarbha and will motivate them to send their clients to this place.

Celebrity Campaign

Celebrity campaigns have become the order of the day. When a popular film star or a sports icon endorses a destination everybody listens. Thus Vidarbha too can give such celebrities paid holidays and make him / her brand ambassador. Either it can hire a celebrity from the target market who has an appeal the prospective market or it can rope in world famous Indian personalities, who have a pan-Indian appeal, to do the same. Making celebrities associated with them can make several themes more interesting. For example, when promoting dance and music, we can have a world famous dancer endorsing the same.

Develop Circuits and Link them with other Known Circuits

It is not feasible to develop all tourist sites together due to financial, human and infrastructure constraints. Therefore, some of the tourist centers should be developed and packaged with other in what we call a 'circuit'. Tourist circuits are designed to give a visitor a variety of flavour on a single platter. The tourism policy of India apart from developing destination focuses on development of tourism circuits. The model can be used in Vidarbha too. In order to dispel regional imbalance different circuits can be developed and can be interlinked. At the same time care should be taken to link them to the broad national tourism circuits. Four suggested circuits are as under:

1. *Nagpur 58 kms Ramtek 127 kms Wardha 12 kms Pavnar 07 kms Sewagram 20 kms Bordharan 65 kms Nagpur*

   Apart from being the premier city in Vidarbha, Nagpur also has Deeksha Bhoomi and dragon palace. It is also a haven for the shoppers. Besides having the famous temple of Lord Rama, Ramtek is well known for its scenic beauty. Wardha has a piece pagoda and close by Sewagram has Mahatma Gandhi's Ashram. Pavnar has a unique concept by the name Geetai Mandir. And finally, Bordharan is a the right place for those who would like to get close to wilderness.

2. *Chandrapur 45 kms Hemal Kasha 15 kms Anandvan 25 kms Tadoba 50 kms Markanda 80 kms Chandrapur*

   Chandrapur is famous for its handicraft made of Bone China, coalmines and Buddhist Caves. Being a part of the pre historic Gondwanaland there are fossils of the great dinosaurs, which again can be of much interest to the visitors. Hemalkasha is an orphanage for the wild animals, perhaps only in the world. Anandvan is a self-sufficient village set up by the visionary social worker Baba Amte. What is striking here is that the whole administrative set up is run by the leprosy center. Tadoba national park is one of the best habitats of the royal Bengal tigers. Markanda temple is called as "Khajuraho of Vidarbha" for its beautiful sculptures.

3. *Amravati 100 kms Chikhaldara 30 kms Muktagiri 08 kms Bairam 45 kms Salbardi 25 kms Ridhapur 18 kms Astamasiddhi 25 kms Amravati*

   Amravati has Amba Devi temple and Kaundanyapur, famous for natural beauty and temples. Shegaon is well known as Vidarbha's Pandharpur and Anand Sagar.

Chikhaldara, a hill station in hiding is worth paying a visit. Nearby is the Melghat wildlife sanctuary for the nature lovers. Muktagiri which is famous for Jain pilgrimage and waterfalls. Bairam is place of scenic beauty and pilgrimage. Salbardi, situated on Satpura range has both hot and cold springs, underground temple of Lord Shiva. An annual fair held during the month of February/March draws crowd from far off places. Ridhpur is the pilgrimage center for the Mahanubhav cult and is also known as 'Kashi of Mahanubhav cult followers' throughout the country. Astamasiddhi has a well the water of which cures skin diseses and temple of *mahnubhav* architecture.

4. *Buldhana 60 kms Shegaon 85 kms Lonar 50 kms Sindkhe Raja 20 kms Rajur Ganpati 60 kms Buldhana*

   Buldhana has Balaji temple and is well known for excavation of statues of ancient era. Shegaon is well known as Vidarbha's Pandharpur and Anand Sagar. Lonar has the largest impact crator in basaltic rock in the world. Another noted feature of Lonar is the star shaped architechture. In Sindkhed Raja there are a number of monument in this small township which owe their existence to Rajmata Jijabai and her father Lakhuji Jadhav, ancient temple of Neelkantheshwar and Rameshwar have great heritage and architectural value. Raju Ganpati is one of the Ashta Vinayak temples of Maharashtra.

Trade Shows

Vidarbha needs to participate in the trade shows both India and abroad. There are a number of national and international forums where a tourism organization can showcase its tourism products. At the same time these since these trade shows provide a platform where both buyers and sellers meet, it can really be an opportunity to bring in business. Some important international forums are International Travel Mart (ITM), Berlin, Pacific Asia Travel Association (PATA), and south Asian Travel and Tourism Exchange (SATTE) etc. Likewise in India Travel Agencies Association of India (TAAI) and Indian Association of Tour Operators (IATO) meet annually and old trade shows. At each such forum a special theme can be highlighted. For example, the stall can be specially designed as a tribal hut and can show case the rich tribal culture of Vidarbha.

Internet

Internet today has become a powerful means of communication. The world can be at one's fingertips. The advantages of internet are many. The prospective clients can take a virtual tour of Vidarbha at the click of a button. At the same time they can post their queries online and be replied in minimum possible time. Thus there must be a website on Vidarbha replete with quality images that can draw the attention of whoever visits the site. The site must have different language options as the visitor can be from any part of the world. Another intelligent way of using the internet services is to post ads at the popular website which when clicked should lead the browser to the Vidarbha's website.

Information Kiosks With Touch Screen Info-Systems

The information kiosks play a very important role in motivating a visitor to a particular destination. It must be a unique blend of man and machine. Firstly, it must have officers with professional outlook who can politely listen to the clients and answer their queries. For the tech savvy visitors there must be a touch screen info kiosk that provide all the information about Vidarbha at a feather touch. Such touch screen kiosks are very helpful at public places like bus stand, railway station and airports.

Tourist Offices Overseas

The help of tourism offices overseas can be sought to promote Vidarbha. They can hold special meeting with the local stakeholders and promote the destinations. They can even make Vidarbha a theme for different festivals organized. However it must be supplemented with sufficient printed material.

Theme Campaigns

An annual theme campaign can bring in the attention of the whole industry to a particular attraction of Vidarbha. It could be the Lonar one whole year followed by tribal life and so on. Such theme campaigns are of special importance as they can hold the interest of the prospective customers for long.

Popular Contests and Sponsors

Cultural Nights. Some popular game contest can be organized to make more and more people aware of the places of tourist attraction in Vidarbha. At the same time Vidarbha can sponsor a free holidays to the winner of various other contests. There are several travel magazines and TV serials that come out with such contests. These contests in a way promote the destinations. Besides the winners who get to see the places can bring in word-of-moth publicity.

The cultural nights have become a big draw in the recent past. The Khajuraho Dance festival, the Konark dance festivals are to name a few. Such dance festival can be organized in and outside Vidarbha to showcase the culture of Vidarbha. Besides it can show case the painting, performing art, music (Vocal and instrumental) and sculpture. Traditional bazaars where the artisans can.

Light and Sound Show

The sound and light shows have become very popular with the visitors from both India and abroad. There already exists such a show at Prerna Sthal at Yavatmal. Such projects can be implemented at other destinations to draw more and more tourist. The presence of so many forts in Vidarbha provides ample opportunity for such shows.

Fair and Festivals

The fairs and festivals of a place can itself be promoted as tourism product. The Pushkar Fair in Rajasthan and the Rath Yatra festival of Orissa are good examples of festivals that have been cashed upon. Similarly the unique way of celebrating festivals like the Ganesh Puja and the Janmastami can be easily promoted as tourism product besides show casing the culture of the region.

Inviting Film Crews to Shoot in the State

The locations shot in the films create an aura around them and becomes sought-after destination. If Yash Chopra's movies shot in Switzerland can boost outbound travels from India to Switzerland, the same can be done to Vidarbha. If films from both bollywood and abroad are shot in Vidarbha it will create an interest among the domestic and international visitors to have a look at the same places shot in the movies.

Conservation Campaigns

There is an apprehension that bisons in wild would soon become extinct and Vidarbha is one of the their last bastions. Therefore a conservation campaign can be kicked off that would save these animals and at the same time bring much needed publicity. The pandas in China were saved from being extinct through this model campaigning. Back at home, Assam has used this model for the One-horned rhinos and it was a very successful campaign. Therefore bison can be given the status of a national animal of Vidarbha and similar campaigns can be launched.

Ghotul–A Unique Institution

Ghotul is a primitive practice that is as modern as it can be. Among some tribal community like the Muriya in, it is compulsory for single men and women over the age of six to be part of an institution called Ghotul for free sex. The tradition is practised to train the youth on how to overcome attachments, jealousies and possessiveness and to instill the idea of community love.

Ghotul is a large hut outside the village where everybody assembles after sunset. The girls and boys pair up after dancing and singing and have sex for five days. After this, if a boy wants to marry the girl, he visits her family and pays her price. If he is unable to do so, he works in her house till the money is raised. If he does not want to marry her after five days, both of them start looking for a different mate. No man can sleep with a woman for more than five days. Meanwhile, if a woman conceives a child, it stays with her. Whoever she marries becomes the father of the child.

A great part of the unity and happiness of the tribe depends on Ghotul. The songs and dances performed in the evenings are mostly sexually suggestive and provocative. However, the final decision regarding the pairing rests with the leader of the boys, Sirdar, and the leader of the girls, Belosa. In order to impress the girls, the boys give them gifts like combs. A wooden comb is considered a gift of love among this community. A good comb collection is a matter of great prestige and the bigger the collection, the more popular is the woman.

Ghotul is becoming extremely popular among tourists visiting Chhattisgarh, and is the reason why crimes committed due to jealousy have hardly occurred and adultery ever committed, similarly this concept can be promoted in the Vidarbha region also.

Challenges and Opportunities

Challenges before Vidarbha in promotion of its destinations are many. Firstly, it does not have the required fund for such a massive campaign. As has been discussed in the previous chapters, this region has been utterly neglected by the state and the central government. Alternatively, the private entrepreneurs are shy to invest in the region since they are doubtful of their returns. Secondly, many of the beautiful temples, sculptures and forts are loosing its charm for the want of conservation. Only when the place is well conserved and is equipped with all the amenities, we can think of even promoting it abroad. Else, it would dissatisfy our guests. Third and the foremost challenge is the ignorance among the local people about the cultural heritage their region possess. Also they are unaware of the benefit that tourism industry can bring about. Therefore, it's a big challenge to educate the whole mass about this. This can only be achieved when a specialized institution comes up with a mission to make the local people aware about the importance of preserving the cultural heritage and make tourism a thriving industry.

The extent and depth of the lack of awareness of Vidarbha is truly unbelievable. Many are not sure about the geographic location of Vidarbha in Indian map leave apart its USPs. If Vidarbha has to create a name for it a massive campaign is what is required. The challenge will also lie in Cultural Sustainability – to balance where information ends and intrusion begins. How much exposure will help the tribals and how much will change their intrinsic way of life. Some of the other challenges are:

(i) Lack of adequate infrastructure in the form of air services and airports, roads, telecom and accommodation.

(ii) Levy of tax on tourism and tourists that are not only high but also unconscionable.

(iii) Plethora of clearances to be obtained from numerous agencies of the Central and State Governments.

(iv) Difficulties in obtaining land for hotel projects.

(v) Restrictions on movement of tourists and tourist vehicles since Vidarbha has many natural sites which are restricted ares.

(vi) Lack of adequate security to tourists to go around without fear of bodily harm or loss of belongings as there is always an apprehension of naxalite attack.

(vii) Inadequate human resource development leading to the visitor being treated more as an intruder than as an honoured guest.

Despite these challenges, there exist many promotional opportunities in Vidarbha. Since most of the western countries have shown their interest in rural India Vidarbha can take advantage of it. Rajasthan has already cashed upon this rural aspect. Similarly, farm tourism has caught up in Punjab and Haryana. Even United Nations Development Fund (UNDP) has funded Rs.11 crores for the development of rural and indigenous tourism. The rural tourism does not need much investment in infrastructure. The very rural life can be promoted in the campaigns. Similarly, Bharud, the indigenous street play can be used to promote tourism. The tribal culture again can be used for promotion. Vidarbha can be promoted as the destination for nature, adventure and eco-tourism.

6

Conclusions and Recommendations

Vidarbh is a region gifted with many splendid natural attractions. It is geographically positioned at the heart of India. It is a region with many unique features. It is a region capable of achieving virtually anything it sets its mind to.

With collective resolve, tourism in Vidarbh has the potential to be one of the most significant drivers for economic prosperity into the new millennium.

Recommendations

Tourism can play a role in diversifying the economy of Vidarbha region. As one of the fastest growing industries in India and the world, it cannot be ignored as a generator of economic activity.

The region has significant tourism resources, and some promotional effort is already in place. However, there are opportunities for broader development of resources and attractions, particularly those related to culture, history, and outdoor recreation. The tourism infrastructure has not been developed to its fullest potential, including the development and interpretation of products and the marketing of those products. An additional goal should be to get tourists "out of their cars and onto the streets" to both enjoy the region and to create economic benefits.

The strategy described below has broad applications in urban and rural areas across the region. The new strategy works via *two* primary initiatives: *destination marketing and sustainable tourism development planning.*

The destination marketing strategy involves coordinated advertising campaigns, promotion at regional and global tourism exhibitions, development of destination brochures, posters and other media, and working with international travel providers to offer promotional discounts on travel to Vidarbh.

The sustainable tourism development planning initiative seeks to promote better private sector/government partnerships to ensure that adventure tourism develops in Vidarbh in a manner that is well planned, sustainable, and beneficial to both the regional economy and local communities.

Articulate a Policy on Tourism to Establish an Agenda and Awareness

The Maharashtra Government through its tourism promotional arm MTDC has made great strides in articulating a formal policy on tourism development as reflected in the ongoing advertising campaign "*Maharashtra Unlimited*". Successful execution of a tourism agenda, however, requires a permanent political infrastructure. It requires state's endorsement and facilitation through the multitude of ministries and government agencies, which have influence over an agenda's deliverables. In the past setting up Garhwal Mandal Vikash Nigam (GMVN) and Darjeeling Gorkha Hill Council (DGHC) has boosted tourism promotion in the respective regions. This time-tested model can also be adopted for tourism development in Vidarbh.

Suggestions

Establish a permanent Vidarbh Tourism Authority Limited (VITAL) with representations from each of the relevant Ministries having impact on tourism to facilitate the development and implementation of tourism policy and programs. VITAL will play a vital role in charting out a path of success for Vidarbh's tourism development. VITAL must lead the tourism development effort for the region and work to enhance the heritage component of its efforts. It could expand its role in this effort by creating a special committee for regional marketing or other special needs as appropriate, or it might serve as the convener in the future to address new issues. From time to time new alliances or collaborations may be needed. A model VITAL should constitute the following

Office of the Governor	Executive Oversight
Ministry of Culture & Tourism	Lead and Ownership
Ministry of Finance	Customs, taxation, currency
Ministry of Law	Immigrations
Ministry of Home Affairs	Police, security
Ministry of Commerce	Commercial
Ministry of IT & Communications	Communications
Ministry of Transport	Infrastructure

Establish a Foreign Advisory Committee to Identify Priority Markets and Advise the Administration on Tourism

Vidarbh has a number of strong industries and trade organizations. The airlines, travel agents and hospitality industries all have associations representing the interests of their members. While both the government and MTDC have historically tapped the industry's native expertise, foreign industry participation has been minimal. This potentially results in the exclusion of the foreign perspective necessary to craft policy and plans from a foreign visitor's point of view. If Vidarbh is to compete for tourists in a global market place, it must have the knowledge of its competitors, its target markets and the professional executions of an international marketing campaign that are critical success factors to the long-term national tourism agenda as well.

Suggestions

- Establish a Foreign Advisory Committee (FAC) within the proposed Vidarbh Tourism Authority Limited (VITAL).
- Conduct a market research in countries from where visitors generally come to India for rest and leisure. Initially it could be members of European Union, Gulf and South East Asian Nations.
- Engage world class PR, advertising and marketing promotion professionals to shape and execute the promotional plans in overseas markets.

Develop and Expand the Heritage and Cultural Tourism Market

There are strong historical themes related to several centuries in the past, industrial heritage, and religious and folk traditions of the region that should be developed into marketing themes or branding concepts to interpret the rich heritage of the region. The region should preserve and develop historic sites, artifacts, and cultural resources. Farm tours, industrial culture and history, and the rural culture should all be promoted on a regional basis.

Suggestions

- Endorse the current efforts of the institutions like Vidarbh Economic Development (VED) and local universities to create a Cultural and Historical Committee. Develop the initial steps to success and monitor and promote future phases of this effort.
- Work closely with entities that are "packaging" tours and events for the region to include heritage and cultural sites and venues.
- Expand and upgrade existing sites. They are generally under-promoted, under-leveraged and under-protected.
- Identify, analyze, and prioritize current sites, their needs and their benefit to the overall programme. Sites related to cultural and natural heritage may take priority.
- Explore options for assistance to upgrade sites including advocacy for the appropriate local, state, or national protection measures.
- Create a marketing and promotion strategy for individual sites and for a regional campaign. "Packaging" sites will continue to be critical to success.
- Work closely with state agencies to provide support for high priority sites and to create the appropriate collateral materials, or include the sites in existing state or regional materials.
- Work closely with existing regional tourism entities to create broader support. The newly formed VITAL can work closely with MTDC and ITDC to include some of its sites in the regional and national brochure.

- Use local resources to strengthen the heritage package such as HVPM which are central or state projects and multi-jurisdictional in scope as a model or resource.

Develop More Retail Opportunities in the Form of Outlets and Specialty Stores

Suggestions

In particular, retail development related to crafts and antiques, historic/knowledge themes, and sports/outdoor recreation would be appropriate. Discourage the development of outlet malls; rather focus retail activities to existing commercial districts. Site opportunities for retail development include former religious-cultural buildings and historic districts. Work closely with successful self help groups (SHGs) to mentor new commercial enhancement groups.

Develop Links to the Natural Resources for Tourism Potential

A natural resources tourism strategy would include gaming and fishing activities as well as hiking and biking activities. This strategy may draw more resources and "customers" to the more rural parts of Vidarbh. Links to the surrounding areas will also be necessary. Currently visitors often stay district headquarters and travel to the rural portions.

Suggestions

- Understand and support the role of cross county or cross region hiking and biking trails, Rails to trails, and greenway projects. Greenways and trails should be viewed as economic development tools. They tie the region together and create a network of access points. These points could be parks, museums, or main streets. Ideas should be linked to both a strategy for Eco or Natural Tourism and to the Open Lands Prioritization and Management Strategy.
- Explore an increased role for MTDC and VITAL in this strategy. How can the region best use/change the MTDC regional maps to serve the area? How can the region link with the larger region?

- Create new links with the neighbouring States, say Chhatisgarh, which may be a new tourist draw.

Continue to Update Information and Entities Related to Tourism – The Tourists, the Sites and the Service Industry That Supports it

It will be necessary to continually update information to stay on top of this growing industry. Current events will change markets and tourists attitudes. New facilities will impact trends and opportunities.

Suggestions

- Distribute new data to all parties and incorporate the information into future plans. For example, TCS is working to prepare a new (1st time) comprehensive, regional assessment of the area. It will reflect, "What we don't have, but need" to recruit new events or tourists to the area.
- Formulate an Institute of Mountaineering, on the lines of Himalaya Institute of Mountaineering (HIM) and Nehru Institute of Mountaineering (NIM), National Adventure Foundation (NAF) etc. Their role will be to identify, coordinate and aggressively market to new events that will fill the "voids" in the current calendar. These will be large events that will use multiple facilities. It will include baseline data to help coordinate events to avoid overlapping events. The room tax will help to fund the participating and helping organizations and institutes. The under utilized MTDC Yatri Nivas will function as the housing bureau. In this case, the goal is to better use what is currently in place.
- Continue to survey visitors coming to region, to determine the types of attractions that could be developed to lengthen tourists' stay in the area.

Develop the Appropriate World Standard Infrastructure to Service and Support Tourism

In travel and tourism parlance infrastructure has three components:

(i) Basic infrastructure (i.e. transport links, telecommunication, energy, water treatment);

(ii) Travel and tourism facilities (i.e. signage, information services, facilitation, etc.);

(iii) And product development options (ecotourism, special tourism areas, health tourism, etc.).

While all three areas may need concerted action, the policies, mechanisms and level of intervention are likely to be different.

Now, India has been keenly focused on such major infrastructure development projects as ports, high-speed rail, highways and airports. Vidarbh too had its share in projects like National Highway Development Project (NHDP). While these projects are critical to Vidarbh's economic development, the emergence of Vidarbh as a viable international travel destination requires the needs of the international tourist be more specifically addressed. The following categories are all critical, tourism related areas, which should be embraced as a national development priority:

- Improve access to Vidarbh's public lands, historical sites and natural attractions
- Application of multi-lingual signage systems and service personnel
- Adoption of international standards for grading hotel accommodations
- The introduction of mid-priced hotels, motels and lodges aimed at the tourist market.

Suggestions

- Fund infrastructure development to open inaccessible areas of potential Vidarbh has one of the most virgin forest areas than any other region in the country. Much of this virginity is a factor of limited access. Vidarbh's spectacular scenery and recreation opportunities have great potential if made more accessible to tourism. The government needs to make a long-term commitment to fund the requisite bridges, roadways, power, water and basic infrastructure needs to open up its forest areas to tourism. Of course, keeping sustainability in mind.
- Establish professional management of national historical

sites Vidarbh has a vast treasure of national historical sites and attractions. However, it generally lack consistent professional management. Its infrastructures fall short of international tourism standards. World class private and public models such as Colonial Williamsburg, U.S. National Park Service, Polynesian Cultural Center, etc., should be examined as potential best in practice applications for Vidarbh's attractions.

- Establish a consistent, regional tourism support infrastructure
  - Expansion of domestic ground transportation systems, friendly to the foreign user
  - Introduction of standardized, multi-lingual signage systems for all airports, roadways, busses, trains, subways and taxis
  - Improvement of foreign language capabilities of those engaged in the tourism industry.

- Adopt and apply international grading standards for hotels The current classifications and the grading of Indian hotels are not always consistent with the standards employed elsewhere in the world. This leads to potential disappointment and dissatisfaction when foreign visitors experience a level of accommodation inconsistent with a hotel's advertised rating. Thus a truly international grading standard for hotels must be applied.
- Encourage the development of a 3-4 star hotel infrastructure Vidarbh lacks acceptable, moderately priced, international standard 3-4 star accommodations. Vidarbh is missing its fair share of this significant middle-income market segment because of its lack of affordable, western standard accommodations.

Cultivation of a Healthy and Robust Air Transportation Environment

Any tourism agenda cannot succeed without the support of a healthy, viable, air transportation sector. Not only must the environment sustain incumbent operators, but also it must be conducive to the stimulation of new capacity. This requisite environment is currently absent.

Suggestions

It is noteworthy to mention the name of AIR DECCAN, which has revolutionized the aviation sector in India. It has provided connectivity to many small cities wherein an Indian citizen can fly with a fare as low as Rs. 500. Another small airline named JAGSON is dong the same but has restricted its operations to Rajasthan. Vidarbh already have domestic terminals at Nagpur. It needs to be upgraded to international standards. Besides airstrips must be developed at other district headquarters. Only then budget-friendly no-frills airlines like Air Deccan can be invited to start its operation.

Support Balanced Measures to Both Protect Security and Facilitate Flow of Visitors

The post September 11 environment has produced a number of changes round the globe, which could potentially impede the flow of foreign visitors to the India. At this point, such balanced policies need to be formulated that not only protect security but facilitate flow of visitors.

Suggestions

A special Tourist police wing on the lines of Delhi and Goa Police is a good idea.

Increasing Length of Stay

More number of days a tourist stays more s/he spends. As such the average number of days a tourist spends in India is high. But our aim should be to keep the tourist engaged in different activities and itinerary so has to increase his/her length of stay.

Suggestions

- Varied itineraries like ecotourism, culture tourism, adventure tourism, tribal tourism, pilgrimage need to be promoted.
- We need to expand international marketing. Current international travellers on business or otherwise are restricted to Mumbai and Ajanta-Ellora. This element might create a starting point for future efforts. They may be lured

to Vidarbh on some or other pretext. This element could be developed during the 20 year vision as appropriate.

Invest in Human Resource

Education and training presents major opportunities and challenges for rapidly expanding travel and tourism sector in India.

Suggestions

- Travel and tourism should have access to government-funded training.
- Education programmes on at least equitable basis with other industries.
- Public education and carrier programmes should draw attention to job prospects in travel and tourism.
- The private sector should also pay an active role in ensuring the maintenance of highest international standards of management and services.

Reduce Red Tap

Suggestions

- Easier entry and exit formalities.
- Single window clearance of tourism related projects.

Tax Intelligently

Suggestions

- Indian destinations, including Mumbai, Delhi and Rajasthan state are ranked among the most highly taxed in the world.
- Future revenue flows will depend on the competitiveness of travel and tourism, which implies equitable treatment relative to other industries and to competing destinations.
- As a key export, travellers and travel companies should not be taxed in a discriminatory way.
- An increasing number of user fees are being applied to travel and tourism–for air tickets, security, airport construction, highways and the like.

Funding

Funding sources could include hotel/motel tax, local sharing, grants, and the budget allocation. Some efforts will not require direct funding. Programmes can be enriched by in-kind services, mentoring or advocacy. In this respect the services of Tourism Finance Development Corporation (**TFCI**) comes handy.

Indicators

The key indicators of progress in this area would include the following:

- Number of visitors in general or at specific sites
- Hotel occupancy
- Spending on food, accommodations and traveller services
- Number of jobs created in tourism services
- Average wage of new jobs
- Business start-ups in tourism and recreation
- Investments in business expansion
- Fiscal impact: urban and rural
- Household income
- New grants for specific tourism venues
- New interpretive programmes or packages.

Conclusion

Travel and tourism must have been the first hobby of the earliest human being. This is because he wandered across the countries in search of food and shelter. Later, with the development of civilization, the motive for travel shifted to business. Since the barter system was in place, he travelled from one region to another to exchange the surplus goods he produced with the goods of other region. Over the years travel became a pleasure activity instead of a necessity. Man no more travels just for business but to be away from his home and explore a new place. The invention of automobile made this easier and more comfortable. Cross-continental travel became a habit with people with the discovery of new sea routes. Today it has emerged one of the largest industry in the world with an annual turnover of US$ 450 billion. To quote Singh (1975), '*modern tourism is a direct product of economic and social progress promoted by technological and scientific advances, higher real income, longer leisure time, demographic expansion and increasingly cheaper and varied tourist-plant facilities that provides the essential conditions for the growth of tourism.*'

Tourism 2020 Vision is the World Tourism Organization's long-term forecast and assessment of the development of tourism up to the first 20 years of the new millennium. An essential outcome of the Tourism 2020 Vision are quantitative forecasts covering a 25 years period, with 1995 as the base year and forecasts for 2000, 2010 and 2020.

WTO's Tourism 2020 Vision forecasts that international arrivals are expected to reach over 1.56 billion by the year 2020. Of these worldwide arrivals in 2020, 1.18 billion will be intraregional and 0.38 billion will be long-haul travellers. East Asia and the Pacific, South Asia, the Middle East and Africa are forecasted to record growth at rates of over 5 per cent per year, compared to the world average of 4.1 per cent. The more mature regions Europe and Americas are anticipated to show lower than average growth rates.

Tourism as a driving force for poverty Alleviation, Job creations and social harmony, has a special significance for India. It provides an opportunity for the government to recast its priority, and look at tourism as a catalyst to start the much-needed acceleration of economic growth, particularly in non-urban India where the bulk of the economically disadvantaged people live.

Nontheless, India has made a tremendous progress in the years after independence. The World Travel and Tourism Council (WTTC) estimates that contribution of the hospitality industry to Indian GDP is expected to go up to 6.6 per cent by 2010 and foreign exchange receipts from 10.8 per cent to 12 per cent of the aggregate exporter earnings in the same period. Given a thrust and determination it is possible to exceed the rate of growth of 8.43 per cent on arrivals projected by WTTC.

Yet another remarkable trend in favour of India is that the average length of stay per tourist (around 30 days) is one of the highest in the world. Moreover, according to conservative estimates, tourism presently is providing employment opportunities to more than 8 million people in its direct sector. It becomes all the more important, since the employment multiplier in tourism sector comes to be about 2.36, i.e. direct employment to one person in tourism industry creates employment for 1.36 person in other sector of the economy.

The first thing that comes to one's mind while planning for tourism development is that why should anyone come to Vidarbha in preference over other known holiday attractions. The answer is, why not – Vidarbha is a region gifted with many splendid natural attractions. It is geographically positioned at the heart of India. It is a region with many unique features. There is Chikhaldara – a hill station in hiding, Lonar – the largest impact crater in the basaltic rock, Markandeya temple – the sculptures of which is no less than Khajuraho, four national parks replete with wildlife, the interesting yet intriguing tribal life, mouthwatering dishes, the best variety of oranges and the rich historical legacy...the list is endless. It is a region capable of achieving virtually anything it sets its mind to.

The marketing jargons eco-tourism, ethno-tourism, niche tourism, high value and low volume fit the bill of Vidarbha market. To create a niche within the niche market special institutions can be set up to encourage the study of tribals textiles and jewellery designs. This will generate interest among the special interest groups interested in studying the same. Similarly Vidarbha can tie up with NIFT and NID for upgradation of designs for the handicrafts so as to increase the unit price of the products and work out a better export market for them. Also specialized museums giving a glimpse of the tribal life can be set up in the tribal dominated part of Vidarbha. The idea is to establish Vidarbha as an independent brand.

No doubt, the main difficulty is the total lack of awareness. But that's both a blessing and a drawback. Since the area is virtually unknown, it's a great opportunity to put theory into practice and to use textbook strategies for tourism development, though one needs to proceed cautiously. Also, you can't blame your predecessors or learn from their mistakes. We're going to tell the world that Vidarbha is the very heart of India and how can one miss it !!!

With collective resolve, tourism in Vidarbha has the potential to be one of the most significant drivers for economic prosperity into the new millennium. As Dr. APJ Abdul Kalam, The Honourable former President of India puts it: "*Our global society continues to face major challenges, one of the most important being the imbalance between the 'haves' and 'have nots'. If the Travel & Tourism industry can realize its full potential, this will make a real difference."*

Bibliography

Mohanty, Pragati 'Hotel Industry and Tourism in India', 262 p. *Dharmarajan, S., and Rabindra Seth* 'Tourism in India: Trends and Issues' South Asia Books 1994.

Chopra, Suhita 'Tourism and Development in India' South Asia Books 1992.

Chowdhury, A.N. Handa, B.K. 1978 Some aspects of the geochemistry of Lonar Lake water. Indian Journal of Earth Sciences, Vol. 5, pp. 111-118.

Bansal Dr. S.P. (2002) Tourism in the New Millennium: Abhishek Publications, Chandigarh.

Chopra Pran (2002) Successful Tourism Management (Vols. I & II) Sterling Publisher.

Fredriksson, K. Dube, A., Milton, D.J. and Balasundaram, M.S. 1973 Lonar Lake, India: An impact crater in basalt. Science, Vol. 180, pp. 862-864.

Fudali, R.F. Milton, D.J., Fredriksson, K. and Dube, A. 1980 Morphology of Lonar crater, India: Comparisons and implications. The Moon and the Planets, Vol. 23, pp. 439-515.

Hawkes, H.E. 1967 Geochemical evidence on the origin of the Lonar crater, Maharashtra, India: Discussion. Geological Society of America Bulletin, Vol. 78, pp. 1199-1200.

Kelkar, Keshav "Rohini" – A Novel: Rajya Marathi Vikas Sanstha.

Bhatia, A.K. (1978) Tourism in India-History and Development (New Delhi: Sterling, 8).

Chon, Kye-Sung, and Michael D. Olsen (1990). "Applying Strategic Management Process in Tourism Organizations," Tourism Management, September.

D'Amore, Louis J. (Winter, 1987). Tourism: The world's peace industry. Business Quarterly, pp. 78-81.

De Kadt, E. (1979), Tourism: Passport to Development? Perspectives on the Social and Cultural Effects of Tourism in Developing Countries; Oxford University Press, New York, USA.

Government of India, Ministry of Information and Broadcasting India: A Reference Annual, New Delhi.

Government of India, Ministry of Information and Broadcasting, Handbook of India.

Government of Indian Annual Report 1999-2000, Government of India, Ministry of Civil Aviation.

Gunn, Clare A. (1994). Tourism planning: Basics, concepts, cases (3rd ed.). Washington, D.C.: Taylor & Francis.

Hunt, John D. & Layne, Donlynne (1991). Evolution of travel and tourism terminology and definitions. Journal of Travel Research, 29(4), pp. 7-11.

Mishra Lavkush Cultural Tourism in India, (Mohit Publication, Delhi-1999).

Mishra Lavkush, Religious Tourism in India, (Mohit Publication, Delhi-2002).

Seong-Seop Kim and Choong-Ki Lee 'Push and Pull Relationships 'Annals of Tourism Research, Vol. 29, No. 1, pp. 257–258, 2002.

Coccossis, H. and Nijkamp, P. (eds.) (1995) 'Sustainable Tourism Development', Ashgate: UK.

Cooper, C. and Wanhill, S. (eds.) (1997) 'Tourism Development: Environmental and Community Issues', Wiley: UK.

Hall, M. (ed.) (1998) 'Sustainable Tourism: A Geographical Perspective', *Longman: UK, Lawson, F.* (1998) 'Tourism and Recreation Development', Focal Press: UK.

Lea, J. (1998) 'Tourism and Development in the Third World', Routledge: UK.

Pearce, D. (1989) 'Tourist Development', Longman: UK.

Ashworth, G.J. and Dietvorst, A.G.J. (eds.) (1995) 'Tourism and Spatial Transformations: Implications for Policy and Planning', CAB International: UK.

Gunn, C.A. (1994) 'Tourism Planning: Basics, Concepts and Cases', Taylor and Francis: UK.

Inskeep, E. (1994) 'National and Regional Tourism Planning: Methodologies and Case Studies', ITBP: UK.

Ravenscroft, N. (1992) 'Recreation Planning and Development', Macmillan: UK.

Renshaw, M.B. (1997) 'The Travel Agent', Business Education: UK, 1901888002.

Kolte V.B. (1996)Prachin Vidarbha Ani Ajche Nagpur: Amravati University.

Deshpande P.S., Sawant Ramesh. (1998) Nakashash General Knowledge Maharashtra Samarth Udyog Prakashan.

Nadeem Hasnain (2001) Tribal India Palaka Prakashan.

Chitale Shripad Keshav. (2002) Virabhatil Koriv Gufa Akshar Rachna.

Fadke Dr. P.N. (1999) Prachin Bharat Wah Vidarbha: Hardas Veena.

Kale Y.M. (2003) Gond Lokancha Itihas, Mendhekar Sindhu, Koyal Sadhna Bhagwat Shakuntala.

Mandlik Prof. Chandrakant (1995) Apla Maharashtra, Sahrda Sahitya Pune.

Indurkar Udayan (2003) Drashta kala Sadhak, Sanskar Bharati.

Tavade Dr. Mohan, Sawant Sambhajirao, Amrute Prof. V.G. (2001) Maharashtra State Bureau of Text Book Production and Curriculum Research, Pune.

Deogaonkar Shailaja (1989) Vaidhrbhiiya Adivasi Jeevan Ani Sanskruti: Mangesh Prakashan.

Karanjkar Bapu Sahib (2001) Amravaticha Itihas: Amravati University.

Vyavhare Prof. M.L. (2001) Amravatiche Sanskrutik Jeevan Amravati Raupya Mahotsav Varsh: Nagar Vachanalaya.

Kolte V.B. (1989) VarhadCha Itihas Amravati University.

Gokhle Shobha (1983) Swayambhu Saraswati Vidarbha: Chitrashala, Pune.

Chitale S.K. (2000) Vidarbha Paryatan Vaibhav: Shubhangi Mule.

Mali K.M. (1974) Yadav kalin Maharashtra.

Jamkhedkar (1974) Pavnar Yethil Tathakathit Vidhivadh Murtipratima, Vidarbha Sanshodhan Madan.

Hirulkar P.S. (2004) Aranya Odh, Rucha Prakashan.

Mule Prithvi (1999) Vikas Paryatan Margadarshika Prithviraj Prakashan.

Holloway, Christopher, J. (1983) the business of tourism, London MacDonald and Evans.

Witt S.F. & Mountinho, L. (1989) eds. Tourism Marketing and Management Handbook, New York; Prentice Hall.

Mill Robert Christie (1990) Tourism: The International Business. New Jersey: Prentice Hall.

Smith Stephan L.J. (1989) Tourism Analysis: A handbook, Longman.

Pearce Dougals (1987) Tourism Today–A Geographical Analysis, London: Longman.

Bouyden John N. (1976) Tourism and Development. London, Cambridge University Press.

Robinson H. (1976) A geography of Tourism, London MacDonald and Evans.

Lungberg D. (1974) The Tourism Business, Boston: Chaners.

Holloway J.C. and Plant R.V. (1990) Marketing for Tourism, London Pittman.

McIntosh G. (1986) Tourism: Principles, practices and philosophies, New York, John Wiley.

Kaul R.N. (1985) Dynamics of Tourism–3 Vols., New Delhi Sterling.

Negi J.M.S. (1982) Tourism and Hoteliering New Delhi Gitanjali.

Usha Bala (1990) Tourism India: Policy and Perspective New Delhi Arashi.

Selvan (1989) Tourism Industry in India; Astudy in its growth and its development needs, New Delhi: Himalaya.

Cunningham A. (1972) Archological Suvey of India Report Vol. 2, Varanasi: Indological Book House.

Government of India, The Encyclopaedic district Gazetteer of India: Ministry of Information and Broadcasting.

Government of Maharashtra, Maharashtra State Gazetteer: Ministry of Information and Broadcasting.

Government of Maharashtra, Marathi Vishwa Kosh: Ministry of Information and Broadcasting.

Government of Maharashtra, Drishtikhshepat Maharashtra: Ministry of Information and Broadcasting, Mumbai.

Government of Maharashtra, (1975) Vidarbha – A way of Life: Ministry of Information and Broadcasting, Mumbai.

Maharashtra Tourism Development Corporation, (2002) Brochures.

Maharashtra Tourism Development Corporation, (2002) Nagpur Vibhagatil Paryatan Vikasa-sambadhi Tippani.

Maharashtra Tourism Development Corporation, (2003) Information on tourist Destination in Nagpur region.

Directorate of Information and Broadcasting, Lokprabha Monthly Issues from 2001-2003.

Microsoft Encarta Reference Library 2004.

NEWSPAPER ARTICLES

Pawar Vijay (01.03.2004, Lokmat), Triveni Snagamachi Athvan karundenare Ambhora.

Pawar Vijay (19.01.04, Lokmat) Vaidharbhiyanchi Ooty: Chikhaldara.

Pawar Vijay (12.01.04, Lokmat) Naisargik Saundaryani Natlele Melghat.

Pimpalkhute Prof. Madhav (01.01.03, Deshonnati) Paryatan Udyogatil Prakashwat.

Chitale S.K. (06.11.03, Lokmat) Vidarbhacha Raigarh: Devgarh Kila.

Sewalkar Ram (13.02.03, Lokmat) Vidarbhala Prachin Vaibhavshali Itihas.

Uttarvar Ramesh (07.08.03, Lokmat) Rushi Munichi Tapobhumi Shrikshetra Tapovaneswar.

Khiratkar Praveen (08.08.0, Lokmat) Bhatala Yethil Jagrut Hemadpanthi Shivmandir.

Dupare Prabhakar (04.05.03, Lokmat) Panyatil Deula.

Kulkarni Dutta (27.10.02, Janmadhyam) Paryatanacha Samrudha Varsha.

Joshi N.M (22.07.03, Lokmat) Vidarbhachya Paryatanachi Durdasha series (1 to 30).

Dupare P. (09.12.02, Lokmat) Sarvadhik Vanasampada Astanahi Paryatanat Vidarbha Sarbat Maghe.

Thavre Prof. Shyam (31.08.1994, Lokmat) Itiyadoh Dhrnachya Saundaryat Bhar Padli.

Pandhripande Sopan (23.11.03 Manthan, Lokmat) Yavatmalche Nave Paryatan Kendra: Prerna Sthal.

Gogte (30.08.03, Lokmat) Vidarbhat Nisarga Paryatanacha 321 sthalancha Vikas Shakya.

Raje Vishal, Kondolikar Nitin (14.03.03, Lokmat) Lonar Sarovaratun Series (1 to 10).

Nulkar Prof. Vasant (04.04.04, Lokmat) Maharashtrian Padartha.

Gawrkar Amod (21.09.03, Lokamat) Satbahinichya Pahadavar mahapashan Yugatil Purave.

Jhade Vikas (27.03.03, Lokmat Vishesh) Ajanta Ellora Leni Nirman Kelelya Sajachya Mahalacha Shodh (Series 1 to 10).

Chitale S.K. (28.09.03, Manthan) Purva Vidarbhatil Durlakshit Paryatan Sthala.

Bhave Madhukar (25.03.1993) Goache Saundaya Vidarbhat.

Rout N.V. (31.07.03 Deshonnati) Vaniche Shri Dutta Mandir.

Aghor Ashwin (23.11.03, Lokmat) Tadoba Prakalp (Series 1 to 7).

Likhr Jeevan (15.04.1993, Lokamt) Khekra Prakalp.

Gadkari Madhurika (08.08.99 Akshar Ranga) Adivasincha Tirthakshetra Hemalkasha.

Chitale S.K. (20.10.2003) Vidarbhachya durg Chakravarti Narnala Kila.

Ambekar Anand (24.04.03 Lokmat) Zhadipattitil Natya Parampara.

Chitale S.K. (08.11.03 Lokmat) Durg Bhramanti: Ambagarh.

Chitale S.K. (04.11.03 Lokmat) Durg Bhramanti: Pratapgarh.

Shivankar M. (10.06.03, Vidarbha Vishesh) Nagzira Abhayaranya.

Pawar Vijay (06.12.03 Lokmat) Vidarbhatil Ek Manohari Paryatan Sthal Shri Kshetra Chandpur.

Chitale S.K. (20.12.03 Lokmat) Durg Bhramanti: Ghanadat Aranyatil Manikgarh.

Chitale S.K. (10.11.03 Lokmat) Durg Bhramanti: Ballarpurchya Kila.

Chitale S.K. (08.12.03 Lokmat) Durg Bhramanti: Bhuikot Vairagarh.

Bhave Pradhnya (09.09.04, Lokmat) Sironchakade Paryatak Akrust.

Dhanke Shubhangi (06.03.03, Sakal) Dagdatun Nighte Surel Sangeet.

WEBSITES

1. www.lonarcrater.com
2. www.amravati.nic.in
3. www.nagpur.nic.in
4. www.yavatmal.nic.in
5. www.bhandara.nic.in
6. www.gondia.nic.in
7. www.gadchiroli.nic.in
8. www.maharashtra.nic.in
9. www.explorewardha.com
10. www.world-tourism.org
11. www.maharashtratourism.gov.in
12. www.vidarbhawani.org
13. www.thehindu.co.in
14. www.indiatimes.com
15. www.travelscopeindia.com
16. www.incredibleindia.com
17. www.census-india.nic.in
18. www.google.co.in
19. www.mapsofindia.com
20. www.webshots.com

Index